response to preverbs

George Quasha's preverbs remind us that meanings ⟨...⟩ a language a stable system; a metaphor is not a murk⟨...⟩ insights; selfhood is not the a priori that enables expe⟨...⟩ ⟨...⟩ ⟨...⟩erally, these poems suggest that, despite our half-conscious reluctance to shed the burden of traditional metaphysics, there are no a prioris, no timeless truths, no transcendent certainties. But the *Preverbs* do much more than provide paraphraseable content along those lines, for they are not so much assertions as events. Read on the page or, better yet, spoken, each of Quasha's lines is an occasion for becoming aware of meaning in the making. Releasing words from semantic routine, reinventing syntax on the fly, the preverbs provide us with endless opportunities to entangle ourselves in ambiguity and seeming contradiction. As they bring us to the verge of unintelligibility, entanglement becomes an embrace and we generate new powerful meanings — not once for all but in a succession of instants that carry us from line to line, page to page, precipitating us into an expansive, endlessly renewable present.

CARTER RATCLIFF
author of *The Fate of a Gesture* and *Tequila Mockingbird*

"Wonder further!" This imperative surfaces in *Verbal Paradise*, the first text of George Quasha's preverbs. I would like to hear it as a call, somewhat in the vein of Heidegger and his more acute readers (say Foucault and Derrida) to think the unthought. Philosophy begins in wonder as Aristotle says, but Quasha reminds us that thought and writing should persist in wonder, pushing the borders of the wonder-ful, being open to the future (*a-venir*), the e-vent, and the stranger, the unpredictable and incalculable, that which will arrive. Such arrivals take many forms and shapes, and Quasha continues to limn the luminal, the axial, the verbal and preverbal. As I read *Verbal Paradise* I recalled Thoreau's extraordinary essay "Walking," which is a startling exploration of the unthought in language and a call to wonder further while wandering farther....

GARY SHAPIRO
author of *Archaeologies of Vision: Foucault and Nietzsche on Seeing and Saying*

George Quasha explores the misty legs of free-space and pure potential, using a wind comb of sorts. *Transfigureur*, he is absorbed in clement metacognition from quick flowing glimpses onto the formless slope, our midsts.

Turning his subtle body in its act evocative of the Clearing, meaning revels in the present~presence, enticed to move. In probing states of address — Quasha — gyro-vectoring, overlapping horizons by way of each focal *haecceitas*.

LISSA WOLSAK
author of *Squeezed Light: Collected Poems, 1994–2005*

George Quasha brings poetry and sculpture to their respective edges—each to its own edge, and by a unique twist both together…. He is an edge master extraordinaire whose gift consists in disclosing the genius of stones to cling to each other at their extremities—at their edges. The same person who balances weighty stones also shapes weightless words. In his aerated poetry we witness wisps of edges that act in counterpoint with those that inform the gravity of his stonework. "Let the stones act on you," he writes, and by this he means act on us both lithically and poetically. The stones act with and by their own dense means, but they can also work their way into language by *l'alchemie du verbe*…. George Quasha's extraordinary art takes many forms, none of them indifferently the same as the others, each uniquely realized.

EDWARD CASEY
author of *Imagining: A Phenomenological Study* and *The World at a Glance*

One might recall that Augustine's deepest probings into the matter of "eternity" occur in his attempt to understand how our relation to both time and what is *not* time are involved in the act of reading a text. *Preverbs* enact within the reader's attention an atemporal exigency through language. Playing intra-syntactically upon the intimacy between time and linguistic structure, Quasha's lines and *fields* of lines fold and wrinkle wavelets of that which lies *under* time. What is unveiled is returned at once to its appropriate obscurity in moment after moment of utterance whose mode of declaration is to provoke the concrete coursing of our thinking toward a certain gaiety of inescapable inquiry. What is suspended across the vanishing interval between a phrase, whose meaning shimmers, hesitates, and sometimes insists even as it deliquesces *within* that interval, and a new phrase, which resonates the first with an ever-efflorescing transformation of sense? It is as if the lion's roar of awakening rumbled forth in the mute but eloquent interstices between ordinary morphemes—where the syllables that carry meanings are *also* vocables merely, but vocables that percolate intimations of the meaning of meaning itself.

CHARLES STEIN
author of *From Mimir's Head*, translator of *The Odyssey* and *The Iliad*

To read George Quasha is to experience unexpected enlightenment. He creates this by confounding our expectations for the order of language that we have been taught. The results are bursts of images exquisite in their simplicity and as profound as traditional Japanese koans. Quasha's blend of the mundane, the arcane and common usage produces a sort of euphoric sensibility; each part a whole unto itself, the atom and the universe all there on the same page. This is an extraordinary accomplishment.

MICHAEL BROD
artist and poet

preverbs

glossodelia attract

preverbs

George Quasha

Station Hill
of Barrytown

Glossodelia Attract (preverbs) is published by Station Hill of Barrytown, 120 Station Hill Road, Barrytown, NY 12507, as a project of The Institute for Publishing Arts, Inc., a not-for-profit, Federally tax-exempt organization, 501(c)(3), in Barrytown, New York.

www.stationhill.org

Designed by Susan Quasha in collaboration with the author.
Front cover: Axial Drawing from the Dakini Series [#1, 10-19-13, 44¾"×40", acrylic paint on paper] by George Quasha

Library of Congress Cataloging-in-Publication Data
Quasha, George.
  [Poems. Selections]
Glossodelia attract : preverbs / George Quasha.
    pages cm
  ISBN 978-1-58177-143-5
  I. Title.
  PS3567.U28A6 2014
  811'.54–dc23
                        2014019793

Printed in the United States of America

for Susan Quasha

preverbs

pre gloss

Glossodelia Attract (preverbs) is one of nine completed books of preverbs as of now.[1] They comprise my main work in poetry over nearly seventeen years. In certain ways they continue the work of decades.[2] When a work persists over a long period of time it may seem to be occurring *outside* time. It happens in a sort of *continuous present*, as Gertrude Stein alerted us. What is "continuous" is the actual *state* in which the work occurs rooted in its moment. This has little to do with the "timeline" in which we see so much of what we do.

Noticing how many times and ways I have mentioned time in the above paragraph I'm reminded of the pervasive focus on time issues throughout the book, and how every line is its own time-journey. It's also a hole in time. Something like a Rabbit Hole into the atemporal. Perhaps poetry is, at least for the poet, the most active threshold between time and no time. I think of a preverb as what gets me there in no time. It's the *when where* allowing singularity to appear.

Walking the razor's edge one can barely distinguish between time and space. Both disappear into the instant present. The tip of the wave is a (non)point of unthinkable infinity.

At an early age I realized I liked books I could open anywhere and find a line as complete as an oracle. The real sense of oracle for me is a sudden indirect incitement to reframe or even recreate reality *in the moment* as, to use bedeviled words, authentic projection. Seventeen years after discovering the modality I call *preverbs* I recall this earlier inclination to view text as handbook for singular entries into revelatory language reality—*linguality*. The present book calls this phenomenon *glossodelic attractors*—revealing acts of the tongue that draw reality into a matrix of new configuration. Neologisms imply there's never enough language to say what's singularly true.

A note on those neophyte words: *Glossodelia*—from Greek *glosso* meaning "language, tongue" and *delia*, "manifest, visible"—resonates obviously and perhaps hazardously with both *glossolalia* and *psychedelia*. In my ear it implies that intense speaking can spontaneously reveal the unknown. Then it *attracts* the mind to further (un)knowing. As psychotropic language vehicle, preverbs can reorient the mind by shifting conceptions of what language is. Unlike proverbs, preverbs never claim to embody wisdom as such nor to transcend uncertainty. And if they're on guard about anything, it's losing their sense of humor.

I should note that the title occurred first in 2012 when Gary Hill asked me to help come up with a name for his retrospective at the Henry Art Gallery in Seattle, and we (including our other long-term collaborator, Charles Stein) arrived at *glossodelic attractors*; the live performance Gary and I gave for the opening was called *glossodelia*. Over the years preverbial reality has insinuated itself in our axial performance, and so it was perhaps inevitable that preverbs should find in these terms a willing consort.

Of course poetry proves next to nothing. And indeed saying all this resolves less than nothing. But then, resolution is overrated. A good punchline is just a blow to the back of thinking. When we get over the stun we realize the sound we heard was another crack of the whip, which, on the positive side, broke the sound barrier and we "become as children" looking up for the jets that gave us the non-local boom. By the time we hear it the object is gone.

---

[1] The present book follows *Verbal Paradise (preverbs)* (Zasterle Press: La Laguna, Spain, 2011) and will be followed this year by *The Daimon of the Moment (preverbs)* (Talisman House Press) and *Things Done for Themselves (preverbs)* (Marsh Hawk Press). A book here is defined as seven "preverb-complexes" or poem-series of varying length.

[2] I think of preverbs as having begun in a poem written in my mid-twenties, "Of a Woman the Earth Bore to Keep" (*Stony Brook Magazine*, 1/2, 1968), specifically in four "Proverbs of Soma" which came to me in dream. Several years later the work became *Somapoetics* [1-58]: Book One (first-fifth series) (Sumac Press: Fremont, 1973) and *Word-Yum: Somapoetics 64-69* (seventh series) (Metapoetics Press: New York, 1974). A complete edition through Somapoetics 99 is in preparation.

speaking animate

for Robert Kelly

The trouble with paradise is you never want to be away from home.

I make what calls me out.
All gone before you know it.

Words may drop passing color yet seeing you here now are born again, and again.
Closing a word in the mouth feels the sound until the tongue can't stay still.

To unmask is to go silent.
Language makes no promise to communicate.

An articulated sound has it own dream in the ear.
Her presence in the room gives aroma to the syllables I voice.

Now she's ready to draw eros from foreign bodies.
It starts by focusing on the sounds beyond hearing, still felt.

By *she* I mean who speaking *animate* configures.
This is the time of alternative obscurities to see through.

Through thoroughly, as a word weighs.

They're playing the perfect music for our movie, *Rushing to Meet Anima*.
The rhythm's spacious enough I slip in the back door without a trace.

The drama is gathering soundless. It lives like that.
I never let go of her hand in my other world.

This I learn from you who read me back.

They say ancient Irish saw serpents where there aren't any.
I descend from there to here where I see what I say even unsounding.

Writing I extinguish my voice but there's calling you hear.

Falling apart is syntactic.
Writing at the edge of collapse is surrender.

Saying depths in a tongue all hands puts the cards on the table over the edge.
Time to stop asserting order where it's already in waiting.

Write this off as of a poet or one inspired by being written through.

A sacred grove takes refuge in the voice.

A language hasn't come through to itself if being inside isn't self-instructive.
Syllable by syllable earwise spreading orders the cells.

What configures signs, time switching subjects on the line like my life.
It seems the same is saying there were no same.

A journey ever worth taking records itself within your hearing even now.
"I will always have been here before with or without you."
Gnoaxial poetics, for want of right naming, finds pulse in grammatical drift.

The more she says the more I find configures.
The new singular noun soon plurals.

I'm beginning to recall the forgotten adventure, long since signed for.
The time of our playing recalls us back together.

This very time turns into space in our search for self true north.
Her tone is dissecting the next move out before.

The tense is two timing us.

The experience beyond reportable experience is self sensing.
Real work is indefensible.

Now to dowse the poetics of the poem to come.

We hold these principles to be self evident — in order to be self evidence.

Configuration is parthenogenetic.

We're talking fate here.

High flying biology. Bios mating logos.

Flowering, percipiently imaginarily auto-erotically speaking.

It sees and knows what it's doing not a moment before.

We call back to our other us through the air pressed into sound.

I'm just trapping animal life in its resound here.

Our group gives the dream time.

A date's charge belongs at heart to anytime.

Our only mythical bird is fleeing the page as we speak.

It makes a very very very fast line out.

Sculpting hands in the saying.

Not every finger is instantly intelligible.

Signing principle, it calls itself, and hands itself over.

Watching your dancing feet is its own dance.

What if everyone talked funny at once.
I'm willing to avoid special pleading but ignored distractions will have their say.

Sudden behaviors may be of unaccountable origin.
Tongue the surface long enough and you bleed old demons long in exile.

Learn from the dog to dig up old shame, then bury it where you want it.
If you find a guy's personality be sure to send it back.

Meet you where we know each other.

Beautiful music takes me away rather than throwing me further in.
Clamoring lines cannot disguise the sound of one mind slipping.

The center is holding just fine, yet the periphery is forgetting where it is

Freudian slips of the hand put your mouth on your money.
Also note paradisal memes at the tip of the slip.

Life goes on ... off ... on ... off.

What am I hearing with these other ears?

Prepare your mouth with pre-carnal intentions.
Poetry valorizes childhood because children make language.

First language.
It gets you little again to be verbal.

I can't deny my excitement upon reaching the threshold of carnality.
No more hovering over secondhand bodies.

The heart is the organ of consorting.

Life is intelligent means it knows where it's going but I don't.
Fearful asymmetry.

Contacting the word's core intent to mean itself is poetic insistence.
Logophagi know that certain morphemes are more delicious than others.

No truth behind the poem, only forward in its own before.

I'm scared sacred.

The threshold of panic is nearer than you think.
I see line as raft on which to contemplate the dangers of survival and not.

Mind turns all day long on feeling good about this or that.
Keep losing favorite images of myself: getting harder and harder to favor.

The earth does not fruitlessly give us her fruit.
Turn your back for a moment and another portion of Eternity is hiding in your mind.

Every forecast verbal order betrays its possible oracle in the wild.
The music undesigned by music is from the earth and feeds undefined needs.

No two sins are the same.
A reading here either tunes me back or unwinds me out.

Incarnation potentially is paradisiacal entering the paradipsychical.
It's time to pull your head back in between the letters.

Poetry marks the passing of time with lived-in beat, wording up and off, bounding.
Every thought rethinks reversing further.

Mind action a pulse felt in the telling's no easygoing equation.
The lump in the throat gets bumped up.

We mean to dissatisfy one tune at a time.

My date with Blake has brought me here.
I write his name now as never before.

It teaches me to do as I'm folded.
Nothing is the way it's always been said.

Working language means cutting through to secret holdings.
My stash of youth is long forgotten.

I have no idea what it is I'm doing, so I ask you to read me to me.
Slips of the ear show me my fear.

Words can lead by op-smart, letter-flicker, and unagreed literalities, you dig.
My goal is to be all here all the line.

I leave the tail behind to lighten the page.
I leave room for the animal's tale to renew.

Slips of the hand make me hear again.
I go dumb to enable speaking direct.

Youth of being is a work in ungress.
Now go home.

"If all is illusion then the distinction illusion/reality is relatively useless."
"Absolutely."

ONTONONYMOUS THE PARTICULAR

A letter is a wand.

A word the bird let loose in whir.

A sentence a neighborhood to let mind range with over to there.

She dances beside herself.

This vision has no outside, no matter how many times it's said.

The pulse is in palettes and feet.

Sound you hear is from the bottom in its middle having grammar.

It makes sense the way it makes love.

I belong to her beside herself.

Tear along the line that has no other side.

I draw her moving as if drawing blood.

Thicker or thinner across the space depends on your pressing in and how far.

She startles herself out of oneness to excite her zero, loving her many.

Two dissimilar objects in the same frame resonate ownness.

The paradise that is not inside the voice has no song.

Imagine a world without first languages.
Struggles of the undertongue are accordingly allowed.

When the poet surrenders long enough language surrenders.

I can't stop my hawking attention to the charged thought entities in evidence.
Torsion saves us from believing where we are.

I want to eat her thought of herself at play in my image body.
I feel so close to her when she lets me say these things.

You should not believe anything I tell about her. It drives her away.
She's getting away! Start over: She *is* getting away. By her nature.

Poetic surprise is saying in which there is no gliding beyond the syllable.
A torqued word in the mouth is nature's tongue tuning.

I watch my hands lose things in plain sight.
The thrill of impermanence is theatrical.

Using your lingual reflex she lassoes your linguality well nigh bronco busting.
The tongue gets kicked around no matter what.

Earth talks dirty to distract me from counting the virtues of my day.
I'm left lusting in the sidelines.

My gender is feeling a little dizzy in here, pronouns adrift.

The path is a sudden curvilinear reach.
I'm on retreat from working intricacy inside the work.

Rushing forward here at any moment it's never too late to return and we do.
I do. I am a man who marries. It's how you say it to yourself.

Throttle the syllable when it asks for it.
It's the emphasis by retraction that gives the thing outline.

It has to deal with sudden emergence you can call visionary, if you see the point.
That's a figure of speech. It figures speaking and long legs ready to curve around.

It channels a further self still off yonder.
Therefore the lasso effect of the text. Suck back.

I can't tell you where it's starting and stopping, it's so life-like.
Enjoy the inevitable disorientation (she's watching from afar).

Confusion can come in pairs.
The number is no help except for the relief. Timely but temporary.

I'm seeing through clouds—can you tell?
Tell me, fold back the lips, there's unspeakable color to reckon with.

The poet opens small doors to her other worlds.

I watch work confusing gender, eroding priority.

A subsequent sigh is involuntary and therefore has keyed force.

I can't wait to contemplate these words at the end of the line.

I'm starting without you.

Contemplate our world allowing that its creator has a sense of ecstatic irony.

Perfection takes off the white gloves.

Clouds part.

Vision is a state in which a god knows you as it biblically were.

Shine through or see through or more.

Every two is manyer than you think and a splitting *y* in the middle.

We fork by nature.

We talk treasure down and dirty.

Till death do us art.

I admit to wanting to hold her hand while crossing.

This first line is an inexact repeat of a line to come.

Given that the earth's not round but spherical it's flattish from where I stand.

You can prove me wrong right now performing the indicative 1ˢᵗ person as you.

Equally true is the question how wrong can I be?

Earth claims person and gender in that we are.

I would know that voice on the phone no matter what.

Earth has a poetics with a noetics.

From ecodelia to glossodelia in single line bound.

In this measure poetry is irruptive.

An unauthorized line tap. No mercy.

This is an instance of a voice trying to get through without giving a name.

I couldn't wait to get home and throw open the brackets.

So much language is forgetting who it is.

Identity is evaporative at a certain temperature.

Language is child's play.

They'll say anything to get the attention saying deserves.

This fulfills the promise of the first line.

Possibly I can't stop remaking the world in her own image.

She is coded to chop logic like garlic.
It's more literal than literary, like garlic.

The line is introspecting upon itself.
How I know is going with the wide awake irreality of indefensible rhythm.

I think to hear what things think in me.
Surfacing against the grain thinking things can't see straight, let alone repeat right.

It tries to come through but I'm adrift in chronology.
Temporal feedback has underlogic.

The time based medium tells its own fortune.

Imagining going on forever without attachment is beyond imagination.
Like rearview backtracking with forward view the very line scans as it goes.

Lineal relation to the whole feeds on a sense of isolation felt in a crowd.
A midline crisis reflects changing subject midsentence with a straight face.

The line can't make up its mind but takes me here anyway.

The resident language is strictly autobiographical.

I leave content to the voyeur in me.
At a certain point in the story only leftovers will do.

My life story is at stake.
I'm left to hovering over scraps.

Poets and children at play love levitating agents.
Protectors of intelligential somniloquies are loving in silence.

Dante, Dante, para-Dante, parasomnial Dante, body of sweetheart.
Soul sought Avernus, spirits are at play like lines at bay.
The tone! The vowel! excited sounds leap from our scrapheap history.
Coffers, coffins, and other commonly sacred confines … think dictionary urns.

A word and her thing are non-separate in real talk.
Dogs bay at spirited sleep talk's diction fictions.
Time to let thinking marry her extradimensionals.

Just think! there are those who think emptiness thoughtless!
Registering the heart on full, champagne all around!

Enough does not readily apply to poetry and sex.

Lexical spaces are peepholes for those pressing from the other side.
Reading is being spied upon, dimensionally speaking.

And we wonder what is running what and who, whom.
Who knew in the big picture with the luminous sky the mushroom has an eye?

Thought forms traversing language dispose by attraction the matter in hand.
Word order guides mood weather.

Miming the poem, so to speak, life aware meditates itself.
I speak in analogy to the extent that things properly speaking compare; they don't.

I don't and I won't compare unless my spine lengthen and the vine stand straight.
A verse is the possibility of prefiguring what is actually happening as it turns out.

Only possible to study time from the perspective of the atemporal.
Poem time wells in semic spaces between, literally.

No telling what it'll tell next. It's not literature it's typing.
Always on time even when late or early bespeaks a throughsexed poetics.

No summaries.

> *Hope to repair wrecked train of thought.*
> CHARLIE CHAN

Why do we want to be the covert choir of preaching poetry?

A soft word does not scratch the tongue.

She feels for you.

Or *it*, what only understands perfection precisely where it is, instantly.

Our minds are working side by side and word by word with breathing spaces.

Thinking listens up in her youthful instance.

Reading between reverbs. Body middles sound sense from the inside.

I is *going* for us both.

How talk it walking? in twos? plus ones?

You can put a poeia on the end of anything and we'll feel it.

Like penile nothing.

If you have time and space for it let it rip right through, readerish.

Reading descending. It's more than a sentence that goes down so far, and you in it.

Highly localized interiority is infrasyntactic.

It tracks language feeling for itself.

I celebrate the wobble in the middle.

It draws out the well of onliness.

Ancient ancestor once say, "Even wise man cannot fathom depth of woman's smile."

I'm feeling by ear.

Consider them gods and not cruel but ecstatic.
They have trick tongues and can't talk straight but use us as waves to curve words.
In this moment we are here for their ride. Climb on under.
Transport poetics in the transtraditionals, revering rumors revved high.
We ask forgiveness for poem talk. I'm on her knees.

She makes me say these things because she is a middle way like no other.

The method is to wear me down to a base line vital pulse.
Next pour right through carefully following the barely perceptible impulse.
Almost dreams the state resists the name but go ahead and call it poetic that flares.
Poetics remains neutral on its name but takes care when it comes to hers.
There's a watch out on her names.

It makes me wait until I have nothing else to fight with and then sets me loose.

When I think what is being said I get a lump in the stomach.
No go on the intellectual gizmo.
Yes on any kind of lift, free run, no drift, too swift, the actual thing getting a lift.
It hits the beat like rock bottom.
The tongue gets hands on quick.

The hearback suddenly gets high in the sense of crossing right on over.

I feel language like a woman.

What you read is what you get.

Easy to forget that even now the tongue is doing its dance of attraction, with veils.

Her smile talking says I'm a noun ready to verberate, so I'm here, on verbal crawl.

Tongue obsession follows radical inflection.

I'm not talking about something so much as reflecting it on bended knee.

Getting reports on language is a thriller.

A thing you know has already said itself, but testifying further is another matter.

Poetry is a life threatening force.

Getting a living chance to come through or not by speaking at the leaping point.

Poetics is indifferent to the outcome but not the come from.

Jesus fuckin' motherfuckin' Christ is now a term of exaltation excited beyond irony.

She kids me not the Magdalene.

Sine qua non of the mind gone sane.

I was not born to sing but apparently I'll risk singing to be born.

The right hand wouldn't understand what the left hand is doing even if it knew.

Fascination comprehends the days falling from me.

Syntax imitates this temporal bind. Ending in the middle.

Open to the end and over.

Opening the mouth lets out the whodunit, to whom who did what.

Birthing grammars.

I'm here on spec.

Some things get said to find out what it's like to be said.

The poetics of birthright is ever in a state of neglect on our planet.

We're sending out for alternatives.

Poetry experiments with the principle that if you can think a better place it can be.

The request comes from language itself bioprogrammed to optimize.

The claim is non-authorizing. It clamors.

The threat is that things will clear.

This in the wake of the words still falling from.

The whole thing said's verb.

Talking hands can't keep to themselves.

From the beginning is speaking on behalf of the truth in its unauthorized version.

The principle is if you know you know.
Declaring so presumes true things get a little early notice.

It's long known there's no sexual balance but only precarious rectification *now*.

I precisely cannot tell you how open I am meaning.
No lines link in the end. All lines do from the beginning.

Where she can't track it I can't hack it or didn't. Would not.
The voice from nowhere says *Confess in reverse*. No connectors.

I'm taking the way around, starting where I came through at the start.
There's an area deep inside that cannot refuse when asked.

Even a little attention attends avalanche.
Shave off some phonemic skin to get to a gnoseme.

It's time to invent reading commensurate to it's own undoing.
There's another side trying to get through wherever we stand in the way.

Coach wheels in old movies going both ways push time out into *our view*.
This is how it happens from then on.

Real life is not outside this book.

It feels to me that what is pushing in from the outside is myself.
The overthere is rising as we speak.

I am I that only can walk my plank.
The poet is the part of me that records the plash. Brave girl.

Born of knowing to know is rising to the occasion.
It figures it has a right.

Why bother figuring out what it's saying when you can't remember it anyway?
Take hold in flight.

The body forgetting itself remembers the world too much.
The face has grammar but hearing won't let me see it.

Declaration has more syntax than ever known and higher stakes.
It goes to the end of time which may or may not be now in the line.

I travel by night when there's not a lot of traffic.
Anything for a little more actual space in wording.

Who reads it reads death otherwise.

CODA

(telltail)

Let there be dark, she said it seems so lightly tunneling.

If you say it twice and it sounds right the door is open for a return.
Mind thunders until you hear perfectly.

No gospel is complete until denied and bastardized in strictly personal demotic.
Example: The one that is two is not a shoe.

As for the two speaking as one, what reading hears tell in the middle voice?
It is not the dark that darkens.

She came up behind to be his power and free him from it.
The music of anything said releases its truth.

For our word order minds what it does.
I sing for the one now going by in your eyes.

There is dark to see by.
Grammar opens backsides to let go who did what to whom.

She says I was *born mouthfirst* in Japanese here translated.
There is no natural speech.

Timing out, outing time, time present and time past, timely as the more they are.
Anything talks funny without listening.

On the count of three, spark.

The dark of which we cannot speak is scintillant.
I stand informed.

That at this moment you're not outside the book has zero metaphoric value.
Gratitude is due for trudging along at breakthought pace.

That axial irony's not contrary to straight across, you can take your tonic straight up.
Tonal tissue bounds the body of two.

I study relationships to know where I stand.
Mirror can't stop reflecting further, so we look on.

Word sites where tone writes.
The mouth knows its place, her place, your place all at once to recite further.

The echo bespeaks alternative intelligence.
It maps mind homeomorphic to the territory leading on, sound by syllable.

A bounding line registers levitational overflow in lineaments including desire.
Just talking the things that hold us together hold true.

It takes time to get young.

real time linguality

I walk my language through.

This is what it said on the way.

I am living in the time of the knot.

More in the world the freer I am.

Where I once said this is just for me now it lets itself be before me.

The sun rises on turbulence in hiding, so spit it out.

Everything about me was wrong is the stand in a story of my life.

I'm longing back to where the present begins.

If I had a story it's longer than memory.

I pick particles of a past that carries its charge in my mouth.

Open circulation of moments is only ever happening in the moment.

Holes in meaning is breathing room.

The new in thought is saying it as it is only now.

Mind floats when not looking.

Sometimes my language tells me who's speaking and sometimes not. Like now.
And then. The *I* I count on asks why so secret.

The actors are time shifting and shape sliding verbial nounings.
Wake up and walk your line.

Grammar is getting from here to there strictly between us.
Identity under open pressure has a mounting weirdness quotient.

Spaces she has been trace pronominally in my world.
There are many spoken people in this room.

Don't be deceived by the focus on two, said number two.
How I hold you in space as I talk is now's other reality opening.

Seeing I'm here hears the contrary.
My thought dangling modifies from behind.

We live here where sense sneaks up feeling for a moistening deep.
A moment aware wants forever.

Tongue cannot help but fork to wrap her meaning hungry legs around the mind.

Mary, Mary, double for the trouble.

Her real time is no one time.

Don't try to look her in the eye.

Fantasy is combustible with kickback.

More in the body the seer she seems.

The tongue secretly licks her words before tipping off the sound.

Returning for the rush the grammar swarms.

The non-definitive lure is by no means indefinite.

Beauties get lost in the faces still knowing me fading.

My flower offering's inaudibly prime.

A world's to read.

Mind knowing itself as you has not forgotten itself as her.

Her words grow sensual through the contours connecting.

Ears rev to hear her.

You can never hide her for long.

Her timing is no one's.

Decommissioning wisdom is a poetic act.

My two timing tale is a knot in the unmaking.
I'm taking my order back.

Now speak it away until it comes back of its own accord.

Everything refers but it never lasts.
I spread my time sweeping round as wide as will.

Living time knots no matter what.

Loving curves without losing grip.
Saying it over retracts in emphasis.

The poem riddles without being one.

The ineffable is what is never heard in what is said.
I pray to be free of the freedom that prays.

Life's enactive otherness asks to be spoken to closely.

Time to repent from making things more than they are, and less.
Hard to believe the real hides.

She tunes to a lost ear.
That's how I know she's there.

I find. I call things as I never hear tell.

Love names showing her high life in the contours.
Her lived time loosens my knots.

Poet mind is sideline reaching back into the saying, *manus ex machina*.
I learn her resident logic in my pervasive middle.

Is it time yet to follow the moistened mind?

The eros peculiar to renewable attachment shows a singular face covertly.
When you don't know who you're looking at in the mirror she's back.

The walking talking present predicts no outcome.
Insightful hovering above her name's riding the horse without resting aback.

No need to translate when everything steps out only in translation.

A sign signs to the other side of hearing.
& never ends.

Lay the words down as stones in the way.

Spread your ears.

Reading from zero doesn't know a thing. Not yet.

The time at hand feels under a shell.

What you see is an alphabetic spell cast in a life left behind.

It sounds like a canyon from the inside.

Saying my self fuses.

Earthbound bottom's you know bliss.

Ears suck in omnidirection.

How the awake moments sliding between events show cracks in the day.

Now to set up shop at the interstices of time.

Any way to save the way saves my day.

The poem is the place where I create myself only as I can be said to be.

So where will I be at line's end? is already over.

The paradox of self-creation felt relieved by the fiction of time in the time of reading.

Life blindsides, always timely spelling it out.

You can't construct emptiness.

I don't feel totally real and then suddenly I'm hyperreal.

Glad to be here on this occasion of the turn of phrase phase fresh out.
I jump on in a twisting syntactic flow to feel the real that feels itself.

What's feeling got to do with it is the unsayable part not yet brought to an end.
Too many negatives cancel out to make the singular positive.

I feel an updraft at the far side of the tongue.
Here on the nearside a new sense is rising.

In time a tongue ties to bear all and everything new.

Don't tell me the pleasures themselves are feeling guilty.
Using up fear in verbal revival is how a thing verberates to save itself.

Language sustains the veil of appearance until further light shows it through.
I am the neither you nor me that she is.

I baptize myself present.
A fall in tone is pre sent.

When my desire overflows at the feel of her she flows over me.

Otherwise why am I telling you this like this, here of all places?
I hear loud and clear only what I can't be sure is spoken.

Rime is for the birds, flying fuel time for words.

My two eyes have their own view from above.
As for viewing in two my split is on the way out.

My other me ur-masochist says *order me*, yet *this* I, me, I'm slipping the grip.
Talking in liquid crystal only now, syntactic knots notwithstanding.

Not everything clears in the light—her skin holds your color before you know it.

Dark vision learns saying things in their difficulty without losing the difficult thing.
The unsayable is the lonely opportunity for the now only sayable.

It reads like a finger catch in the thin walls between us, and gets away.
If in time it doesn't teach you to read it it's not written in language.

Now my thinking persona is thinking herself again over yonder where I think to be.
The hidden crystalline potential of water—that's how she makes me dream this.

A line leading the stream takes me over, edgewise.

I'm learning to toggle from state to state and no map.

My vocabulary is doing this to me.

There's to want that doesn't know what it wants.

It only shows up suddenly simultaneous in head and gut.

Its greatness lies in that you can't stop it.

You are its inside, topologically speaking.

And every surface thing said, every dread, all your dead, find new voice there.

Another face feels your face inside your face.

Epic attentions on the lam and wondering who's still coming through, it starts.

There are too few names to accommodate the swarm.

A new math wants to be a me. It's already more.

It knows itself enough to form a furrow here where I'm learning to follow.

Sex in the head in a new way and a new day.

Who knew the rooms could be *another more* and even before your wanting.

Who knows where you are in the self-appointing guide in view.

The only before is what is still unsaid.

I dream I'm entering her cave writing in another tongue but it's not my dream.

I've spent the night tracking an endless winding root of responsibility.
The earth is hairy and can't think without forests.

There are jokes in store for us, I can feel an early rumble in the stomach.
I'm on watch and keep awake reading the signs now ready to talk.

Codes are tracks in the snow and spring's on the way.
Before you know it there's a no show.

But you can always sense the planetary beast beneath breathing.
She lives therefore I think.

There's a register of voice that calls back no matter what it says.
It's what in speaking knows it is heard.

Hearing surrounds the mind waiting to get through.
The idea is to follow into the forest.

One always steps out on a new planet with the same foot, but it no longer belongs.
Love here's a resonance at high intensity, never still, and beyond still.

Language forgets itself, and makes no promise to be here when you return.

How can we live at the edge and no point resting?

The breaks make for right timing.

No telling where it's going. But I tell you it's going. I'm going too.

Language looking through itself sees in real time.

What talks back from the sheer question held in mind?

It screens from view wherein it views on screen.

Laughing without object is saner than it sounds.

Eiron is a god who forgets his own name.

He won't let identity stand up when called, performatively indicatively *divine*.

Myth time follows the bouncing ball.

Music enfolds word by word, right here where it goes.

It slips edgewise with gravity and lift.

What is real for me goes undercover until it speaks for itself.

Already audible is the claim that can't be made.

Calling her love secures the inner edges of certain words in seclusion.

I scry to hear her syntax in folds.

This is not a place to be alone where connection speaks in the bounding round.

reals within reels & other sides

for Carter Ratcliff

The true map lights so many lines no way to follow but staying in place.

I pretend there's discrete knowing yet this arises from unacknowledged links.
I say hear me out but whom do I address on behalf of whom? *Clinks.*
The sadness of texts is a focus of necessity, so where to go tremble but here?

Language tells who speaks covertly whose secret no code-breaker detects.
Its wave in the air masks a flow by way of the ordinary but the clocks nod off.
Just by passing through your mind it seeds the gap to come.

But who dares say what happens in dark places?
You climb air by rising through yourself precisely as no one sees.
Built to rise here on the inside and not a soul to tell.

Middle voice is the voice disclosing the other side of identity.
It doesn't make you go away, it makes you forget there's anywhere to go.
No show but this show.

It's as if the knob on death's door is a warm handshake with an unearthly grip.
The audience you fear died the instant you thought them.
No shaking the ass that's already shaking.

Loneliness with a view. The will to rush is drifting away.
The world you always wanted spreads out with abandon in the denser invisible.

]I wave my hand as I'm saying *waving* and the hand is drawing this picture, it's real.

Setting the sun free in the brain lets a thinking shine in surround mind.
This is not a technique but a high-velocity turn with an urge to tell.

Thinking continuous surface is thinking itself.
I fell off an unknown side in a present tense situation and landed here moving mind.
I reached the other side and realized it's this side.

Listen, there's clinking in surround.

A thing is said on its own plane wherever it gets its information.
Desire recurrently urges us back, fearing loss, wanting what's missed, loudly.

A wild dance of syntax barely shows on the other side of willing reversals.
I feel myself going forward but the direction appears arbitrary.
Yet we always know when something is before us in surround world.

Anyone refusing to make sense until sense makes itself is in self-avant-garde mode.
The sociology is that no one dares admit a free-standing truth.

In the dark of public light what cannot not be true hides from sight.

I'm here to tell you in the middle a story that has not yet told me mine.

We live in a time of the end of the world as told.

It comes to itself without your knowing which end is up.

Pretending wisdom is what is now disappearing.

However ancient I am in my self-destruction wherefore I am.

My startled tears tell me I'm feeling something I don't know.

This is not the place I recall signing up for.

The tell-tale Mayans have a time all their own.

Take it or leave it is the first meaning of calendrical return, a choice is at hand.

Pointing resolutely in no direction there the site itself is turning.

All symmetries retain their power for themselves alone in the turbulent open.

Lusional plays to the unkempt ear bioprogrammatically legit.

Slips of the tongue follow the same old grammar but clang on the walls of sense.

Where do our fictions go when we file them outside the real?

Creating a new world according to *the world* suffers the split.

Never stop trying your inner grammarian's patience to know a tongue biblically.

Once it teaches you to read its way there's less and less to read.

Still, I don't deny feeling the planetary heat at the back of the neck.

Skywriting, wings in flock, clouds picturing, paging.

Given the commitment to say only what is given our dire gaps can only be given.
Makes you wonder what it is you have.

I accept the webbed authority of the unauthoritative evidence before me.
This does not include my saying that I've said so, even if I say so.
Saying the more or less less that is more is a further more.

It's legal as far as it says, by what law is there to tell.

Always looking for the referent, a hand around the air around what's going round.
Feeling refers immediately.
It jumps out of the thing it gets into.

Making no promise to communicate lets more in the surge at hand.

Worlds in creation cut loose by any means necessary.
Geology is the strangest pedagogy.
The footloose knows bottom up.
2012 is a quality of stride.

Bottomlessness comes to the surface.
It's what can be said to do.
For my part I'm stepping in holes to feel the riseback.

I speak running my hand over a bounding surface.

The saying passing through imparts the pulse in place.

What is it you know that is only known now hands on.
Not a question but a sudden declaration of interdependent instantiation.
And according minding mouthfuls are on the go.

I suck on one straw in the shake, now seeing the wet slip unwinding serpentine.
How you touch in on the thing determines how tall the tale.
Anything ever told true on earth is possibly one dermis down, so sign on in.

The very hands that mutter in sleep bespeak undertimely table tapping feedback.

The body tells you what you can say, but not what not.
It says itself all the way along. Slips of the hand and all.
Clasps, clinks, cliticalities, clinal knowledge.

The tongue inclines to the word getting through.
Its desire pulls from a self-veiling liplike presence on an incline.
And other technicalities of clinamancy measured in a longing slide.

A delectative torment of constructing the unconstructible's protosexual aberrance.
This is one of its names on the loose with a paging finger in mouth.
Sounding its own way knows it biblically as it were her.

12.12.12 slipped by as if it never was to be but in a fearful symmetrical dream.

It teaches itself life likeness in an unexplained current setting free the foretold.

When the ahistorically temporal meets the atemporally historic, well, this?

Cf. the poetics nightmare YOU HAVE REACHED THIS LINE IN ERROR.

Messages from the deep can creep.

There is value in following belly first.

Accordingly I put before you that I come before myself.

No line leads back to the world it has never left.

It is kind to ask a thing what it wants to be in your mind.

May your entelechy run me through.

I stand insurrected.

The giving time of the millennium is a return to sender.

I am post postmaster with a difficult delivery still shorn in real time.

That's tongue signing for *the ancient message is born post readable.*

The return of mind is out of reach.

The forecycled world's white canvas awaits the feminine touch.

Signing off … on … off … on …

Letting go in charged time is to be where you are in the cross-wide view.

It's awkward to say what really's happening in places like this; it comes out torqued.
No pages skipped, no lines blinked, no need to step outside time this time.

The marriage of true minds, the matter of millennia, the secret subject of poetry, &.
Now we go inside the circle of make believe where we've lived since the beginning.

Why can't Yezidis get out of a circle?
Break the line and spring the trap.
Logic is feelgood cognition.

Ones that fly and land and ones that write and erase are trying to be each other.
The evolutionary gesture is the intimate action taken where it never knew how.

We've come to piggyback the impossible flowing through.
Ladders gone, time to climb.
Everything tells, nothing is trivial awake.
Thank you for the flower although I took it for a weed.
I'm still ingesting cross-sensationally, right where I am.
Divergent moods, modes, souls, tales are from certain angles indistinguishable.
I'm always getting ahead of myself but I've devised this to pull me back in place.
Way back in.

It's the timing of when the time comes.

What does not grow upwards but it grows downward plants in mind as in earth.

I look at it that I thought this project life up and aim to keep it up beyond my days.
The tangled bank of evolving self-interruption whorls through the Broca area hot.
I mean to say what it means me to say.

Mind verbs between all and everything.

No knowing what you know without not knowing, you do know that.
Undertime registers time as its own memory forever happening just now.

A dark mood is a deadly mode.
How many did you stalk in the mind today?

I pull further desire from your self-veiling presence.
I figure you're naked on the other side of your words.

I ask myself: Are you so attached to gender you don't know who she is?
Sucking the referent's so primal, what's to be done?

It's time to take her word for her who says her.
She with whom sex is self-instructive beyond known, unforgiven at large.

Forgive is to hand yourself over gut first.

The breathless sky outpictures itself in my mind where I never keep up.

I wake speaking from the inside of a fresh bulb.

Leaf talk is a declaration of primal variety.

Morphos at large with their logos on their leaves.

I know you when I hear you whoever you also are.

Looking into this intimate world brings it to attention.

Poein is layering up that sustains its impulse unto sustenance.

Clouds hunger beyond even their greatest names, *floccus, uncinus, intortus* on air.

Earth has long been eating me with my blessing.

Anything said without precedent rouses her faculties to act, especially the mouth.

I just felt my stomach think what my head could not.

Skin and earth are drawn to mirroring, here in their moment of truth eye on eye.

Earth genders away from me in our excitement.

I say what senses an ear is free.

No calling down gods but hearing them is irresistible.

The shell telling on the temple to temper Neptune is a species of ancient music.

In the surviving state of attention there's no time to believe what sounds us out.

Once you start going into the corners there are corners everywhere.

My conscious net catches you at this moment on its outer writing edges.

I go fractal in the fact of you letter by letter.

This tracks us only at the points of contact, hence the linear unstorying drive.

We're this far down in the fortunate fall.

Minding the gap gives verb to the released.

This is dimensional unto itself [may I break this shell in saying it so].

You slip out of my hands when you accept their affection.

You can't describe a vision that won't stop for you.

The net forehears your *possible* that we meet like this.

When in doubt I turn to the thinking that sees me coming.

Rooms I ignore flash me spaces in this big inner surround of my head.

The lingo sounds alien the more it goes around.

It comes from afar only to sound like nothing before.

Who am I if not a resource in use at a locus diffused?

At this site the narrator has been nodding off.

I feel formlessly informed right up to the edge.

Grace shows where I am no more failing to acknowledge even in my dark.

Clearly nature that fresh cling abhors a vacuum and does no such thing.

You like the above cloud are not where I see you.

The line is not the reading in place.

It pulls back before the thought strikes home, animate.

It animates.

What goes through you anywhere never leaves you.

You let in and you let on.

The writing is not *my own only* telling me what I don't know is thinking.

I sense bird need to break through the dome of ordinary.

I say it badly to honor its alien nature.

Living is to make the other happy, the other happiness.

It never knows to be right.

Raptor or rapture it rarely cares to welcome.

Asking is masking.

Its line feeds crossways between what has been written and waits to write.

In short its voice of terrifying angels is a poetics of standalone tongues.

In long it has no face to show until you figure it.

Masking asking.

Keep in mind that I speak only from my blind side.

I'm two faces, no, I'm a vase, no, it's how I talk.

Looking down at the ground is more than a headache.
I love feeling my brain knowing itself mycelium gone global.

You think you're in a tangle but in reality it's sensing you whole.
The river runs through you.

Talk to the wand, the tree hand, the flowering arm, the cast of mind.
Immediate classifications long to return to the sea, dream nature.

There are scarcely any nouns making it out alive.
The crazier it talks the truer it moves.

Time was impatient today and wouldn't stay long enough to destroy the world.
If it were a bird its name would take you by force.

The two sins: failing to doubt and doubting.
Here in the middle we find our peace in the eye of the storm.
It minds us here just like this.

It sees not I.

I fall into a swirl imagining the verbs to come.

If I thought to stand straight I'd break, but dropping from heaven I'm gravity strong.

Now I think to take a break from the fall of man.

It dawns in me that this is interluding our ongoing heading downward.

There's an echo in here, nearly.

The after frisson is a sign of life speaking on its own further half.

The tinge of an other voice is enough to perk an ear in hiding.

I elude my familiar to get past a past.

Just think of it, all that moving of the tongue for the never before.

An end to the relative immobility of verb as we know it.

This is to give the missing prelude to the already happening not yet located.

An elusive itch englobes my non-local intimate surface.

It takes every one of our innumerable senses just to address the *drive*.

Any plumb line knowing what the working does delivers shock.

Not only a place to run eyes over succulent saying, but at least it's *that*.

Ditto, ditto.

The horizon is a line of self-consuming sound waves you surf with naked reading.

Suddenly the present erosively summarizes what went before now moving on out.

The times are on the go.

It's by my flaws I find the courage to address from this angle.

It's a mistake to give voice to those other selves, my noisiest.

Hence the power of saying what is so as no one sane would emulate.

That said, the peacock is free to feather me with eyes of threat by charm.

I'm hearing an echo across this stage.

Background music is what you don't hear immediately in the relationship of words.

The poetic is born haunting its future houses.

I project being the voice that cries for its wilderness.

The interested angle is the speaking that hasn't thought itself through.

There's all that could be said that isn't said that wonders what it's saying now.

Our trying sentence types commensurate to wearing new shoes know where to go.

Breaks in thinking induce a ground level fluctuation in the life loop out.

O holy lack.

Beyond the point where the mask attacks its own nature is the raw of my dreams.

A bardo between any line and a further retains a rough of earth, a pulse, *phet!*

A flutter of thinking is perceptible at the distance of a page turning back.

Holding to our edges induces oscillations, frissons, and the effects of walking beside.

The primary ecstasy of keeping alive has been poking through the gaps in the lapse.

A grand resound is expected and equally inaudible.

The authority of the speaker is going too far, I ought to know.

Some fear absence of the figure, some miss the personality, and where am I in this.

No hole, no donut.

Poetry is language saving us from being right.

Otherwise I could never have gone into politics.

I found the other side of the issue on the back of my head.

Without avoiding votes how could I keep this office?

I scare easy on behalf of my constituents.

If you think you know the level I'd watch my feet.

It's that damned impersona.

He never takes his thumbs off the glottis.

It's rarely clear whether certain lingual configurations are threats or lures.

Has Satan got me by the tongue was an early theme before the presumed voice.

Before the throne, before the dawn, at home in her arms, my longing, other figures.

The great three is following but number has found its wilderness.

There is no number for alone, not even zero knows itself that well.

How do you know it's real but that it won't stop talking.

This is neither more nor less important than that I won't stop breathing.

The ambiguities in identity are strictly personal.

You'll never hear me saying we have to stop meeting like this.

I love not knowing who you are any more than you do.

The point of three is that identity pivots in the middle.

It needs room to play between.

This is its poetics, the play in the gears, the view from the rear, tears, seers, leers.

If I were deaf you'd see my hands in the letters building her house in these trees.

You see I've let her in at the poem's request.

She sees me on the bringing end that calls you to the singing end.

I'm not here to do the singing.

Sequence is the read on the pulse.

Stories are born where they're found.

And the rush, the run up to the rumble, turn of torso, sex scene, rectifying signs.

The handle has been removed on the emergency brake.

How many times have I told myself to check the slide knowing the risk.

Interpretation is a lure disguised as a safety rail, but the clang, the clang.

All I ever lean into the downdraft for is to hear her voice clear in the bell, her tongue.

I'm here today honoring the sacred spot of a vacancy in mind.

Being called here is that origin is a perspective we can no longer afford.

To be in the middle is to be willing to lose track, trace, face, pace.

I'm stepping over the words on the way as if stones on a tongue.

It takes everything I have not to throw my arms around these *things* still talking.

A word is a gong.

The big leap is from the lithosphere to the glossosphere with bios inbetween.

I make sign to the brainy mycelium underfoot under time.

It gives the lift only certain sudden glossemes rise to.

A pulse is no more normal than it happens in time.

There's a mind event that knows it comes from the back of the head.

The knot sets up in the center. Time to enter.

It's what can't be said anywhere but here, now, the precise disadvantage.

It would make no sense that it makes no sense but that it does.

If it's not self-sensing it's senseless by attraction, and it says it with noise.

I find it necessary to remind myself at times that I just work here.

The torments of poetry rise again as delights and delirium.

Like any music hearing is first from which reading is born.

Birds get high on honored seeds and return on high.

It's the inevitable imprecision of the determination driving words to new heights.

Pearls before swine has a Buddhist incline.

A new species of magical practice is born every moment is self-proving.

That these several lines were thought in sequence is not a vote of time confidence.

What it sucks from the earth is local only to itself.

Anything written anytime in its morphically resonant sphere roots new on the spot.

My unknown other doing the talking seems to understand my need for never saids.

Immediate time consciousness is a comfort zone.

Better the pain you know than the devil you show.

I know it's good when it makes her laugh in me.

Beyond this quality is a stranger with a strange fan.

There's a species of reading what stands before you requiring a rearview mirror.

Front and back are far from absolutes that comprise the present moment in time.

Now back to you.

Reading a line through tells you if it's talking to you.

There are no shortcuts between hills and vales.

Absolute certainty is kind of unfamiliar.

Nevertheless we have a relationship.

Language cannot respond to inquiry into its nature without feedback from you.

This offers a clue as to why we are in this spot.

It's not possible to resist present disclosure 24/7/365.

The present peels of necessity.

I ripen my own seeds so to speak.

I pivot on my own arhythmic caesura.

My comfort is the art form of the indecisive.

Naturally I hesitate to tell all.

What's most intimate I'm hearing from afar, tide turning, flowback, no wait.

You don't want it both ways but it is.

What's present is ultimately inevitable.

You think you've said something but it's only a beginning.

It's very simple whether it knows it or not.

That like attracts like & opposites attract is par for the course in the real created.
Direct truth is unspeakably difficult.

It's the unidentifiable familiar voice that holds you on the line.
It's unmistakably itself.

I go at it with everything I have and it still gets away.
I'm left with my arms around a charged emptiness yet feeling feelings never felt.

It almost feels good yet it's beyond hard to know.
Indecision where no decision is called for is an alternate reality.

These secrets from the deep are not truly secret and there is no deep to speak of.
We seem to be drifting but in truth we are gathering as the body breathes in a fall.

Alternatively we are dancing in silence and conversing with noise as greater good.
A new formulation in the moment is a future unveiled.

Any stripping down has an eros.
It seems dark in here but eyes are in surround and everything open to visibility.

It's hardly a matter of style that no name comes forward but literal force in letters.

Here we are at the threshold of a new ending.

I'm hooked on the excitement of being what can't just be me.

We meet at stage center and overhear our gossip in the dressing room.

And only come back down to hear the earth pulse on all fours.

Thinking self as primordial is less sin than overstatement.

Strange to find out intelligence is in charge in shadows of my wishful projections.

I only found out about my stage life when the lines got good.

How did intelligence come to mean I spy but fear of the other in its cold?

Language keeps trying to tell us reality's forked truth one word at a time.

Untold numbers, how many unheard lies can I dance on the head of one true thing.

Purpose is for the birds and poetry oddly is their no fly zone, but singing yes & no.

As I go. They go their way also by word of warp.

They sound as swords swerve toward the golden throat, i.e., *metaphor as cut* of.

I offer the pieces I'm in.

Failure honors refusing to name the self-evident.

Mind doubles in place of title, last resort of resource lost.

The difference of tangle & weave is tonal and textural and in time textual.

I get caught finding. I free up evolving to be found. I lose track in the woven wild.

Soap bubble density of the bobbing thing is integument enough to get it to talk.

feedback from the periphery

Waking up's like a bat out of hell.

And how can I maintain independence of sense except as it sounds afield ?

I question the mark that tells me I question when in fact I only speak in question.

Time to acknowledge that the languaging of truth is not behind but ahead of itself.

It proceeds as it were tongue first.

This is a posture like the difference between monkey and man, spinally speaking.

They get high differently and neither can stand lying about on the ground too long.

They're all about acting *up*.

In a world all action there remains an *own* way.

I leave the trees to the eyes and the rare arms around.

There's discipline in disinclination, no leaning into the fall but directing the fall *in*.

Getting a grip accords to the branching, a soft hold between swinging and breaking.

I pick up on the fall in simulacra of my own principle.

Embracing my empty feeling squeezing gently oscillations slow to know but saying.

Overhearing is the only proof.

I detect the scientific method as far as the eye can see.

We have different modalities of being everywhere at once, hyperlocal unendingly.

My date with the daimon dream drags a questionable entity out for questioning.

How do you know the thought is new when you haven't had it?

It says so?

And who's that saying what I haven't yet heard?

Eventually time exposes its centripetal attractions.

I sense critical mass following me everywhere I go.

Common things are on the verge of blending with the unknown.

I live loving in the contours still believing the world launched in the gendersphere.

You can feel when the words feel in place, their calm in your stomach.

They say *lighten up* and I'm a bulb.

The desperate hunt for wisdom blocks out the areas most suitable for vanishing.

I don't understand a word you're saying lit into my fire wire.

Set the mother tongue free from birthing the world you know.

I turn my back so coming words display swarm intelligence, aeroplaning into view.

Sounds of *hilaritas* in crossing tongues, swords, and other dissipative moods.

I'm never ready for resurging hyperbolic syntax curving away from itself.

But it's the best transport for recombinant voices of continuous co-involution.

And other feedback from the flexing surround.

I'm here tracking the loss of heat which is considerable.

Language is conservative until otherwise.

Fundamental is the tone in the timing top to bottom.

I fix on the motivation to catch on to something feeling real.

Breaks in the followable notate the rough of earth.

Its heart flutter in my thinking is only perceptible at the distance of the page.

As I've said before I'll say it again yet it's still not mine.

Breaking the addiction to stages instantly locates the rhythm of the instant.

Swirling through the cracks and flopping into view, is *real* the real word for real?

Accordingly this is further evidence of its hyperlocal address. Reality flutter.

Going in twos is the longest parade.

Bigger numbers start here getting a foothold in attraction traction: *step out.*

I declare open and vast the space before three.

The broken promise of one speaks in a transfinite voice.

Anything has a calling known or not.

It counts and it doesn't know how.

I know how to be tired enough to have nothing left but listening.

My work is not experimental, I am. Yet it works me into the me who says so.

I'm realizing from tone to tone intransitive to the end.
Hyperfinity is your own singularity reflecting on the other side from where you sit.

I'm not your mirror nor you mine yet together we mirror hopelessly diverse.

Wise saying here is limited to preventive prolepsis of any and all self-defense.
This is an unprotected way of checking in on my inner biodiversity.

Self-exposure can't help affronting public morality in nature's way.

Confessing the predator at heart in recovery this life forth is a vow in process here.
Impossible to monitor it as progress vs. regress, may be time to try congress.

Survival of the luridist.

Leaving out the verb is suspicious. Language is a verb. Buddha, verb. *Verb* verbs.
Say it enough and it's appropriately meaningless.

It poems to make the mouth self-moving.

Here we come in on the aspirational act of being useless.
This is the fate of grammar.
A pale fire lights our way beyond the notion pale.

It's what gets in between the words that turns the mirroring neurons on.

The poetics is language feeling oozing through what's never dared be thought.

Too crazy for these cramped conditions.

Concealed inside are the calisthenics necessary for the critical turns.

The self-instructions are sadly flawed by overweening truths.

Turn here just in time.

It's shaving a bit closely for such an unstable testament.

The element of surprise is distributed.

My mind has to go hyperlocal just to feel the full force of the startle.

Thinking has awakened in a vegetationary tangle.

To find a word for the berry's sense of fall while keeping biblical is not proverbial.

A saying for the feeling of peeling from inside the banana takes hypersexual focus.

Who will hump the hemp to prove interspecies porn?

Plants are coming *for* us between rainforest and home front.

There are rhythms in backfield as yet unheard.

Unmouthed myths still hunting storylines in the tangle are trying to taunt.

No merely human mind is ready for this.

Readiness is nothing in a nutshell.

It's back to that sense of falling from midway in the fall.

To take sides in reality in the present makes dizzy in the *actual* sphere.
Any she he it foresees here just to get where it is awake.

It seems you have to have been somewhere near for the line to get you where it is.
Instruction appears to be after the fact while in truth it's running alongside.

It's about which way you face when the oncoming's in surround.
The sphere exfoliates as the past turns out.

I find myself obsessed with form from the perspective of inside preverbal swarm.
The sense of ending is provisional and previsionary.

The bell keeps ringing with no one at the door like a last scene in this movie.
No one is at home who hears it yet we do, beyond question, it pierces in silence.
I'm getting sudden glimpses of what it might mean to know it.

The voice starts to sound polyglotal as in acts of knowing biblically and polygonal.
Terrible turns are in store in the genders. Things meaning what they say.
Look inside just right and they start to come out.

At a certain point in the odyssean winds earth takes you by the tongue.
You find yourself with verbs you never get to use.
It sounds too soon to be gone.
Foregone is a half rime with four gone to mean foreseeing coming out.
Now we are five, where the lines are spoken like a true plant.

I can't seem to help starting out not knowing where I'm going or what it's saying.

I love science and science loves me, present thought donor.

Reporting from the tangled thicket of shaded gender is a vegetal verbal gradient.

The self-mangled text alters the mind reading as eye-of-storm intelligence.

You think it's the other way around and then it is.

Cyclonics in place of attitudes.

Yet thinking in threes as well as trees can have the calming effect paradisal.

I inflect the scientific method as far as the mind can be.

Learning evolving is lying intertwining in the celebrated tangled bank.

This is the planet earth I'm interinventing as I go with the radial flow.

Now to learn to welcome this strange world with open psychesphere.

It's living language when we share it speaking in latter-day foreign mother tongue.

Clear vision at last midway in the fog of our lives, so turn left now, inclining out.

Walking with ex-ray feet to see as I flow, downunder.

In the place of attitudes this goes as far as the mind can tree.

Hoping to skip my reader's inner archive of cumulative interpretative angles.

Now read *angels* for the hell of it.

Likewise Buddha is a verb you never get to use.

I'm seeing *visible* means *can see*.

The son is rising. So? Mirror neurons on the loose.

The reader seeking reflection as in the mirror finds no one in the house of mirrors.

It doesn't take a trinity to strip the psyche bare.

As you hear it you fear or tear it.

I believe what I see as precisely as it sees me.

The earth I love attracts my crazies, so seize me by the ears and be done.

If there were a point we'd have felt it by now, but fire rages radially.

Someone has to say sorry for divine failure. Consider it done.

This slightly alters the fact that it's as naturally unending as it is upending, *crossed*.

I let the thought lizard cross my foot and don't scream.

The famous power spot is the space of any trace at the notion horizon.

The differend goes underfoot in undertime.

Denial subtracts, holding on uses up, delineation won't line up.

Secretly reading wants my referent, but it's forgiven.

Self-forgiveness turns your self inside out gut first.

The poetic moment skips what is beyond redemption, patient for actual return.

The fact of just being said drills through to planetary othersidedness thinking.

This is how we know we're feeling on edge.

So, payback is reflexive.

Dreaming a bird of paradise and the feel of her body on my shoulder, I rescue warm.

It takes a whole body to feel a single thing.

Life is from the stars but it likes it better here.

My job is to let the continual overflow of meaning out of its cage. Seed time.

Death's door's one-sided knob faces in, *fiery*.

It takes a while to find your way around big closure.

I stumble on a whole in a dark passage through.

One touch and I know my body whole.

Saying the parts, saying *whole*, as many as moments are, leaves the whole whole.

I does the speaking part without a version taken under.

This is the real me. Who said that? Maybe *what.* Crossroads.

I seem to know outside the show.

But I still don't believe it. There's flutter.

Without a doubt it's so when it says so.

This is the good part. The real goes feral.

And it still knows its place.

And the weight of the moment in the end, no context, no contest.

With no verb every word verbs.

Once fate, now it can play itself out.

As I was writing the words said this is where life knows it takes place through me.

Sudden turmoil, another meaning's rippling across everything I've ever laid pen to.

I'm surfacing. Resurfacing. New face facing up. Surfing for face.

It helps me see through time to get to seethrough time.

Better to bumble along tongue-trippingly lest I miss what I've been blocking.

It's got rhythm of the third kind. Maybe the fourth is pulsing in undertime.

I take instant refuge under the self-warmed blanketing.

It keeps me present through the mid-winter haze, safe beyond belief.

Anything getting through is already beyond believable.

Cold as hell? Can't get that specific. It goes back and forth. I'm on a swing.

The middle naming of everything is what can only be said between.

Being the medium is getting to the end of the line without ending.

Listen up, the tongue is moving, life is listening to itself.

This is what it says it comes here to do.

Say everything as straight as it gets where it is, in layers, all around.

We let ourselves keep getting swept back into the spiraling in the midst.

It takes a lifetime to navigate.

And to break the fall in time.

sleight of scale

for Steven Goodman

To begin is to be just before knowing where you are.

I get excited feeling my world conception dissipating under my fingertips.
Smelling soil's reminding the seed to seed.
The stream flowing out of the right back brain sketches transfinite geologic pulse.

Forgetting is life editing.
I didn't know till now I don't know on purpose.
The heart beats provisionally.

Certain present needs reflect then flare.
The beat goes on self-gratifying, you can feel it like a member.
Then you remember.

Their beautiful faces are memory traces riming mind back in actual throbbing.
I embrace light in being transparent and I know a visage never quite goes away.
Yet the hold has no source not here.

It could be said more simply if it were simpler, but the view is up close.
It's the micro-movements making me mellow with a threat of wallowing through.
Trance conceals stance as the eyes drift seeing the thing real.

Only the oscillation keeps us waking.
The readable signs are true in self-opposing.
Language breaks itself to be let be.

I feel it gnawing to create itself in obscure laryngeal crevices, so darkly personal.

How do I know I'm here is the kind of question never to ask not looking for trouble.

My inner detective is on the loose but still tracking, yet never as much as it's lacking.

Riming mind is time on the lam.

I have standards but they won't talk to me.

Today is the day I almost know which aperture I slipped into Earth realm through.

Pure poetry is interdimensional deadpan.

I was about to lose faith when the jugular caught on to my soulful jaguar in hilaritas.

Yoking the joke as spiritual activity takes aim for paradisiacal disability.

We went wild to name more gods.

Talking to yourself and talking to your mind can mean something different.

Get it all said in every breath.

How long the line or the life is the time of the hold in the telling.

Long enough to be spoken to by you don't know who blowing through.

You can't give it the otherworldly quality it already has to capacity.

Give poetry a break. It still wants its babble as in the happiness of Babel.

Now take back the allusion to leave room for provisional illusion. It lets speak.

The closed lips awareness cruxes in the contact of pen and paper, so to say.

Writing is the membrane tying in two sides here along the one.

Fuel is the lure to turn into curves of an unbearably beautiful living body.

I end up with my hand in the earth and weeding for jewels.

She refuses my reference.

I'm here with unreferable body and soul. *This protocol is this long.*

The going personality doesn't bother feeling personal.

It's playing both ends with feet on the ground.

Touch tells you one surface is not one mind.

If syntax of Dr. Moebius can't tell itself from the bottle of Dr. Klein, what's a book?

Where the sounds meet and turn around — and around — and stay herewithin.

The whole is what the verb reverberates.

I begin because I can't find any other place to be but here.

The place at hand as a vision of itself is no tautology thanks to your intervention.

I show up to listen in.

Poetics is not a medium but an angle of incision.

Interspecific access neither starts nor ends on a side.

A double negative never stops reversing; the present surface is peeling back.

I and we singular go in together alone to where we only are.

It's reading duty time.

Finding out how being outside everything still wearing your shoes intimates a you.

Another *one* with no additions. *That can't mean me* is a first best thought.

It's everything you ever wanted said but didn't know until now.

One [emphasis mine] non-exclusive of any number is telling.

It's showing through faceted, flayed, forsaken, foregone, flown away, back, at once.

Thrice born is thrice shorn.

Loose to the taste, rough to the touch, heat sensing, crying outloud sounding one.

It was not it before you knew it is not it makes me dizzy. Senseless, sensual.

I saw Dante beholding Beatrice in the Starcart, or so I say what I saw.

I refuse to let you believe me, too dangerous, for soon I would believe it too.

Whatever I'm doing is not to amuse even when *it*'s amused, as it is, just this once.

It hits you in the face, like they say, but it doesn't stick.

A steady state of changing state makes a statement like a question.

Not your face, not my face, not anybody's, until it hits.

Fractal timing times speaking scale after scale after scale, it's as much me as ever.

Ever is equal to never + the other way round, as possibility doesn't have to happen.

The self saying shows through everywhere it can.

It's not my job to know where we are, says a guide self from the other same side.

Only the thing at hand can afford the grip to open the door in *this* way of life.
The truth is lip first.
Secondarily I gender in the wild.

Now for the consequences of the choice to be.
Where's the verb to let be but in hiding.
The lore's a riding: all the names of history are raring to go.

I'm on show as the horse in figuration as if life takes practice.
Reading is absolute beyond the limits of your patience.
Free to mean is glossodelic attraction in the fractions.

Reality shakes off judgment as you shake out a sheet bearing this message.
It gives us to think the unthinkable and the mind to mind.
Here, catch. Where to? Who cares. Realer than ever. Come again.

I'm trying to keep up with my parallel sentence just now writing out the thinking.
This is as real as it gets.
Now is not going away as far as I can tell.

Who knew you can take it as it comes and it'll tell you who you are.
Streaming syntacticals cut grooves you touch to talk identity.
It makes one feel like one.

Telling you forges a focus not otherwise.

Anything has a tone in time and changes as it tunes.

It tunes to you in your tuning.

The fruit never leaves the tree even as you eat it.

I eat trees, I drink people, music sucks mind in its listening, now metaphor is literal.

The leap instructs the groove it shadows.

Hearing is backwards.

A word that means too much is a crisis in the intelligible bearable.

Castration is bi-gender and starts with inhibiting the tongue.

Singularities in discourse are not embraced with fully open ears.

What I can't say language says for me.

Self-vision is not that there's a self but turbulent self-knowing can see itself.

It's not that worlds collide but the horizons of separate worlds coincide *here*.

I missed the flap of memory exposing raw inside flesh but it shows in a far flash.

It gets personal at the horizon where one's own extremes reverse.

Words double for us.

Earth is the mind that can never be made up.

Loving living, living loving—what's the difference but the *i* I make.

Mind does not intend to be understood. Nor tongue.

The flap forward is a fall with grip.

Would I know a starcart if I saw one? Yes.

Speech lack is not tongue lack.

Time is in a knot and it's telling.

I'm doing the speaking like doing time, the twist in the timing.

If only I could get a line on the green fuse driving the vine that motivates.

I know that *it* has lost more referents than I have admissible desires.

This is its uncontesting value.

Each line from the center moves further from the center, and here we go.

Geodelic outreach is obsessively sexual on a planetary scale.

I have a call out for living fractals to join our team of trackers.

Invariance is exciting.

It gets you everywhere as anywhere.

A line is a focus of writing on a scale that invariably attracts alternate scales.

Not ambiguity but ambi-directionality, all your selves as any selves speaking at once.

I'm reaching between the waves, her ocean legs, facing in, spreading the word wide.

Antidotal anecdotal doubting the thing we seek is holding it away.

The fractal wiggle is the way each turn willingly exists through itself.

I scale along telling time from one finger catch to the next insertion.

I've got my eyes on the verb outfront, afire with not yet knowing.

True for one true for all maps the way through earth wishing.
Not to burn too fast she teaches the heat flowing in the step. *Step.*
Over the edge with just enough distance to land in the footstep.

Next like the foot the tongue goes first and not too fast.
It stays the longer it lasts from place to place.
I save enough face for the music in the moment.

I follow the trail as a line I read, so slow it almost moves the other way.
A voice comes up before the next word starts like a throat inside the throat.
Doors fly open in the isolating word: time to go through.

You don't know where you are, it says, and you're not who you think.
Life's still getting used to you.
Intellect's talking a better game than it plays, so watch your hand.

An object in this space cannot depend on its light, god knows (= no one does).
It makes me write two-handed with one pen — what's that sound?
You hear me hanging back from getting wise.

Here to learn the art of forgetting … even what it is this is.

I always know the time and may ignore it.

The time I tell is the place I read.

It says here carrying irreconcilable times inside means pregnant.

Up close has no end.

The realer literal is in letters. Fusion. Minded sound.

Touching down in the lingual absolute mindingly times a place to be.

It reflects back at you upskirt and you feel real enough to inflect through her.

Saying *earth* warms the mouth like *lifting belly* is reading in bed.

It can barely be said without heat encircling the navel.

Speaking linguistic sexual as momentous patois talks your way in deep.

Don't think because syntax dies syntax is dead.

A living body bones up.

The holding's in swing.

Identity means the same swivel, time and again, invariably different.

Even this sentence will rise from the dead not dead.

Mind knows eternal in pulsation. Call the people!

The beat goes back to where you say it for yourself.

In every true speaking gesture time is eroding.

Sooner or later we'll see it as it is, empty.

No sooner, no later, but always as is, edging on not at all.

Yet every moment's longer than seeming, here in the eternity of not knowing.

Everything said has a frame unavailable to itself.

The art sequesters in the quality of trust.

Touching I feel touched.

Can't stop trying to say the feel of mind along this curvilinear no-sided surface.

The force of bounceback amidst rubberbanding gnosemes.

I say let's rest up on the outer planes of the barely intelligible (talking to myselves?).

It makes sense I sense.

Aphasia as technique for making space, these desperate tactics of life intelligence.

Keep getting glimpses like the blowing curtains showing what can't be seen.

Another side is always trying to get through.

What drives it? the pressure, the lean on mind, pushed in on, talking, talking.

I'm had mindly.

Did you mean kindly?

I mistook you for myself, an easy one to make.

What you heard I said is said but not by me.

I take to tongue — that's how it talks!

Mind can't help the rime.
The lobe robes.
Watching time to get an eye on myself and a rough sense of syllable drag.

This is how I count, from midline to the ends and back.

Music is neither a way out nor a way in but both at once.
Nostalgia for the free state before I knew the meaning.
There is no momentum but mind fractals on the spur, timing.

I trust the sense of contour, tracking the tangle from the inside out.

Just because it doesn't come in order doesn't mean it isn't.
This thought is from yesterday which is to say a certain distance out from here.
I'm waving and I'm catching the waves. De*piction* by sound.

I back into the interstratum where non-repression meets non-obsession.
No more self-recognition for me.
Orientation on a möbius plane is bottom up.

I say it to push it out past the said.
Leaving out the verb like not picturing the hero opens the present to presence.
Back to the unsaid, raw desire, the feed.

The species doesn't progress but it leaps out.

Take a line between two empty ends.

Like me thinking of her, the connector between, trait d'union with an onion, whirls.

Translation: thinking this now is formal for me and waiting for you.

You bring me into question, formally speaking.

This miraculous fact is born hungry for the attention it is by being here.

Slow leaping up and down and around and about and on through's a way out via in.

The word vagina is hot.

I distance as I speak even as I burn.

Now I can say vaginal earth is two-way and get the feel and still have no clue.

This is a soft landing on lethal terrain.

Survival takes pull.

I'm paying attention to the feed-in.

Logophilia comes to mind: the lusty proportion in taking verbal hold.

Its variability is scale invariant.

No holding back. And no holding *on*.

In the middle is the swing.

It's difficult to bear that every step has absolute force.

The text requires that you realize your own seduction.
If it's anima you want she's here to project you.
She offers self-protection as self-induction.

Don't pin me down. Identity is an open book, no index, missing pages.
The voice up close alters hearing.
The writing instrument performs the edge of the sound of the mind in the voice.

It's a daring dare to take it as it comes.
Include me out. *One two three poof!*
Take the it off the table. It has a feel of pure alternate reality.

The mood is sudden that everything you meet feels *off*.
The claim to know what you want to say is an incursion.
In a flash I feel projected. I fall on.

Now for a momentary break in self-deception.
A line is an immediate opportunity to self-induce.
What if this is never read except that it is reading out now…

As if to get the *it* back in it kicks its own door down.

There's an eye in iris that's more than it sounds.

The garden has closed the gate on explanation.

All day I felt my lifeline the midpoint between existence and non.

I stand projected.

I always seem to be waiting to find out who she really is.

She keeps telling me she's telling me.

Read the hand you speak to.

It changes as it speaks.

The sexual thing haunts eternity.

The mouth finds itself working out on the labial surface a letter at a time.

We're trying to get slow enough to slip between transproportional worlds.

Use it or lose it but don't refuse it.

Main problem is it gets to be a problem not understanding.

If the flower is smellable where is the ability?

I'm never the same when I hear these things.

The speaker is busy being transparent.

Adam ate an apple but Eve ate a rose.

Too biodiverse to know the language in advance.

The point of dowsing is getting oriented.

Kissed goodbye in writing she pulled me out.

Hovering above a luscious garden of vulvas taught me I was dreaming.

Understanding doesn't travel well from thing to thing.

Inspiration is keeping on track with indeterminate endpoint.

The real experience is not an experience but the waking place I know displacement.

In fighting death ego fights to the death.

Out here on the plane of distinction I'm camping out.

The only discourse in situ shows what's been missed.

There comes a moment in the night I convince death to meet me halfway.

If I go too far along the ecstatic path the mother tongue stops driving.

Duende's a hyperpresence: no name's a good name, dying's bright in the telling.

The only meaning left is the one that wasn't there.

What just happened to me?

This tells me I'm on my way.

Thanks for returning my call.

Things are coming home to themselves.

The flowers are giving their side and we're behaving accordingly.

A name tames but seed has no contrary.

Man in his image fell god.

Who doesn't like to tattle on the creation?

In some realms of the real shortcuts are the long way round.

Impossibility limits beyond limit.

We can only afford to make deals with the unavoidable.

It makes the status quo more interesting than it deserves.

Word is always a verb when you get all the way down to it and on through.

It acts upon you with unreasoning force.

Seed zone.

Life has no contrary; death is a parallel.

Language itself does not oppose.

The lake licks the shore.

The lady of the lake is the name licking itself.

It gets wet just listening. Slow flow.

No voyeur no show.

Knowing biblically is the sacred path.

It's how many ways we take in language and what counts as orifice.

It flows through what's open.

This site of transducing self-identifies me.

The music of what is thinking declares in the flow.

Word orders and world orders distribute themselves accordingly.

Reading is a mystery and we read mysteries to remind us.

The sentence is the delayed knowing long enough to keep enough of us here longing.

No motivation no life. This is an evolutionary fact.

The poetics of the continuous discontinuous is the frame evolving.

Death calls back but I can't recall initiating the call, so rushing on.

Language is visionary before me; using is proving; memory is not primary.

Certain mind figures once released persist whether remembered or not.

Hail to the book which to read is to leave it through, thoroughly, tellingly.

Delight relights.

Babel signals the first cry of singular signals.

Biodiverse language is mind-degradable from zero.

Never leave your zero at home has a feel of motherly advice.

The hunt for intelligent life is what life intelligence does for itself. Reflect. Fun.

The abandoned zero sucks out all from behind but activated it's hyperlocal. Vibes.

Empty pleasure-seeking is imaginable, free reaching.

Evolution by attraction awaits its poetics, no end delight.

In and out of this state it looks at itself in its double mirror incommensurable.

Fresh women in a swing, impossible scent, the music of wings, Priapus gazing.

Self-inducing hand in hand is seeing between bodies and no seduction necessary.

So little time and so much to hear.

Symbols are half handfuls. Seed time.

Logophiliacs know gods spam and no one's listening but us. And *them*.

I offer my arrogance to Mistress Death for only she knows it as gift.

When I give out it will not be for giving in.

Caving in, no; no icons on cave walls; loss is not personal here; I'm still on.

I'm saying things because I'm hearing things that hear back.

Hopping words like freight cars. Streaming.

Coming to the end of the track being a poet means willing to hit the switch.

My body doesn't believe there's a right time to cross so it turns on call.

Listening is not only forward, it pulls around.

Contacting a movement with inwardly configured body lays bare raw need.

You get to be who you never think to be.

It's time for images to be birds and their fractal tracking.

It has come to this and is still coming, the shakeup's auto-syntactic.

No blame.

It furthers to have nowhere to go.

I find myself feeling things in surround.

The streams are everywhere with their currents and their musics.

They instruct in substance seemingly.

Looking on flowing the body knows why it doesn't believe in regularity.

Liquid crystal syntax is that streams hold beings in further patterning possibles.

It doesn't add up or stop adding.

It's more in the more that makes more of itself.

Wanting is that every word opens on a world in open address.

Lacking is the site of desire actually right here.

It is taking the turns it learns being here with you even now.

Gratitude is due for your further streaming.

There are no modifiers as you know everything modifies.

How to say it in language heating breathing being's everywhere barely surfacing.

You want meaning? The thing said is still bare but it's coming to.

The resting point is exposed, the aught is out of the bag.

Holding together moment by moment is only suddenly overall.

So familiar and you don't know what you're looking at.

You know when you've been told.

Insubstantially speaking we're finding our say otherwise.

Tripped up it knows how to be where it is.

Power leaks from your own voice.

In the dream she said like the muse, *poetry is the passion of art*.

She said it flat.

Memes hunt your genes down and fuck them.

"I work toward immediacy," he said.

Atoms spread their subatomics so you get hot meaning.

Another way of finding the threshold is backing in.

A pulse per finger is the laying on of.

I hold from you what I am holding from myself.

Now let me say everything slower and slower to the point of near non-forward.

It takes radial focus to know what's moving and not.

This is still my other language.

I don't yet know its laws.

Its writ of garrulous corpus restores the rights of the all sounding tongue.

It's not mine until I open my mouth unthinking.

This is unsustainable discourse arising in the failed spaces in my speaking.

It gets her excited on my behalf.

I know this by going where it goes.

The truth of time would panic us if there weren't so much of it.

A search in obedience is a search in permanence, so it remains.

Wisdom saying is erosively symbolic language and yet it feels so good.

Yes driving the stake through Dracula's heart is self-staking.

What in god's name is this? but god has no name. I didn't say this even if I tried.

What words do in speaking is erode.

It makes space for the body of language, the rime of the tongue.

The voyeur is on a hunt for the raw.

Playing doctor with the earth.

Reading *between* gets you down on all fours.

All those remembered sins are lessons in thinking.

Time to stop pretending I'm not still pretending. Thrones & unthrones.

There's the feeling that doesn't know what it is, so it comes to you.

Free feeling is free running in free timespace.

The rhythm is the contour of foot and world underfoot.

So much too little time is a sign of the timing.

Now we know that knowing what time is is knowing what time is not.

The end of anything is exaggeration.

Poetry is language scaling to the intimate moment.

I've said this never before in the sense I'm saying it now.

If words were metal they'd rust in your mouth.

I object to the language of object. It never quite doubles for itself.

A poetics of Freud is that all murder is mistaken identity—the object is oneself.

All poetics possible to be invoked are versions of the self selving, like it or not.

How we get to say anything is news to me.

No news stays news.

Otherwise it would cohere as always.

It toughens you up on straight saying, the breakfast of champions.

Eiron is the voyeur god watching over our overfeeding.

Between the actual meaning and the apparent meaning is this meaning.

God is another name for what never goes away. Trouble never goes away.

Therefore nothing follows reliably.

Logic is sudden or not at all.

I'm in love said the sentence to the word interfering with it.

I felt virginal until you read in me. Going all the way.

There's no going back not more forward than you can bear.

The space between revirginates until you rip away the tissue.

Unlimited painful ways of knowing you're here are nothing next to our coupling.

For anything said a further anything talks to differ in and of itself. Not alone here.

It gives you the feel of knowing what is being said in our common darkness.

Its poetics is *if not everywhere at least anywhere at once.*

What is between us doesn't yet know big or small.

Saying scales until it fails. Invariance is not indifference.

For every edge a scrape is telling.

A sharp shift, a shape short—the urge still pulls you on.

A *lineament of ungratified desire* traces in the grain of the voice.

Tracks at the midpoint of being and nonbeing are everywhere at once.

How can I listen to what comes through this blind, deaf, dumb down called fall?

It listens to itself for me that I know knowing has its waiting.

This is the interim. The hall of reception in the time of deception.

Somewhere between wanting to live forever and or to die yesterday, *glimmer.*

Dig the hole deeper, hit water for its reflex.

Already on the other side makes everything urgent.

Everything is itself so far down elements don't know their names.

ins and outs of neverbefore

for Gary Shapiro

This life encased in story I'm holding at eye's length.

An organ form stands behind the telling.

Only the ear-and-spine double curving knows the way around it.

I hear myself thinking how good to avoid writing as Venus mind trap aflare.

You can't catch mind in the lie it's never without.

Note that it goes on without my permission or yours.

I hear it asking if I like its drift toward mushrooming mind.

The mind's pants are always on fire.

It tells you what it wants you to know but not in a way you can know.

I have a call out for a poetics of self-intervention when not looking.

There's a hyperlocal fire brigade that listens to extinguish.

The M on mind stands for more, mushroom, many, moon, mattering.

Mind the poem lest it close on your hand.

The lie has no name you know.

I've told you everything I can tell you without your being already told.

Except this.

The thrice-told tale forgets its name.

The future is the remembering.

In the beginning as in the end, middle is losing track to order on the spot.

A poem meditating on poetry is nothing like a poem about art.

And this is neither.

A body is posing as a poem.

It takes a good picture. Point and point.

Orgone tempest in a teapot. Clay posing as physique. Build in process.

M as in *m*ind is like X only *m*ore so.

Missing is the mushroom long forgot.

This is the perfect place for me, all the free spaces are open on this end.

Interesting is how M has avoided meaning meaning.

Suddenly I need a poetics of too hot to handle.

Take mushroom mind as it takes you, into the pit of scrambled communion.

Decode? Not on your life. Erode? On your life.

No build-up to suddenness of knowing. Build down, tear up.

Mind tricks which is not to say linguadigitation. *Somebody's out there!*

Who can feel actual weight the very word holding sway, heard here.

That's *my* question though not the other's, the one who lingers in the unnoticed.

What clamps the day down behind your back fails to face in the round.

The intricacy of neverbefore keeps the mind at bay.

Intelligent wildlife has you surrounded.

Renegades know on their own, in the end nothing can hold you.

The small dark cell of eyes-closed text is scratched to surface.

This is what it looks like in an altered literality.

It bleeds out, to tell the truth.

Slaves of the future arise you have nothing to lose but your mind confining.

This just in over the fear waves.

Nobody really wants to be present all the time, it screws with the mind.

A refrain like a heartbeat, excitably variable.

An organ refrains to form like bounding line.

When unhappy it pounds the ground with its puny rimes.

As heat does not rise but rushes to cold, spirit squats in poetry.

There's a leak. Hearing a hiss makes for talk, serpentine feedback.

It's as useless to believe in miracles as not, lest they not be as they seem.

Nevertheless I hear Blake slighting the inner slaver while loosing his syllables alight.

The dark trek has its music and grafts.

Its timing turns time over to cross histories. March of the apple trees. Tulips.

Reverse engineer the devolution.

Counter-etymologize for seed syllabic rerooting.

Revise origin.

I'm listening for the music that drives you off the road.

It takes crashing to find the neverknown entrance.

Entrancement by untrackable pulse.

Babel's first cry of singular signals sign for their unborn contraries.

Bad form makes you do what you're not willing.

Reason's the wrong toolbox for what needs to be known in me at this hour.

Dark flower. Imagine eating it whole.

I know it's change by the distance I can hear.

The ear scales by tunneling.

So life catches a glimpse with ungrasped options of view gone vast.

Lingual halls open on both ends abolishing the line of thought just now calling.

Who's that you say you are?

I'm feeling too round to tell.

The work honors desire to take the past to bed and get up from the other side.

The sex of the totem is known in the lift.

It gets biblical from beneath.

Spread flat out—body maps.

You don't get your power from what's next to you—gods, flowers.

Sit hands down touching flat—I'm face up, at last.

Alternate lingualities map as they go.

She dreamt Kotodama the spirit of language descended into sound freed by her lips.

Poetry is language learning to mean every crazed word.

The writing pulse breathes heavy in the pages.

The raw god enters the word it must soon abandon.

Only by letting the loonies out can a mother tongue restore your speech right.

The goddess is the girl in the tights.

If the thing said isn't still speaking it was not fully spoken.

A gnoseme is a word willing to enjoin its deepest secrets even at this late date.

A sign with potential to return whence it comes, in your mind now, first time ever.

The surrounding mood is performative injunction. Seed time, bija rime.

Imagine a word emitting a scent never before experienced: is the meaning the same?

It is speaking past capacity.

Suddenly we're moving toward a wonder in the process of being withdrawn.

Its language takes place in the here that is never not elsewhere.

I'm here to tell you it's sculpting the wake of its current path.

The voice is producing objects seeming to sing to keep present.

The lyric is *do it.*

If the subject is who says Do it, *who are you?*

So much happens the sooner you see.

Saying tangles.

My moment not your moment only is fragile as thick webbed crackle connects.

The truer its name the more physique.

It leaps through hoops to get to the next word. Nest word. Vaster wording.

Born from the mouth it opens.

My language is talking to me and what it's saying is it's not my language.

Too many mycelia linking to too much other.

Some thought grows better by starlight which is distantly older than ancient.

The slides between meanings are evidence of lingual dream thinking.

Sculpts you hear are at behest of the teeth.

They create things hard.

Even the scalpel has a matrix and is said in the cut.

A slice is a separation of identity.

Listening from both sides reflects fineness of the walked edge.

Keeping track where there's no track and no one leaves tracks yet echoes curve on.

There's duty unnamable.

First heard ever is what is heard first now.

Writing does not resist the desire to cross the distant horizon.

No full stop until being born returns from the overedge.

Bottomless memory is behind obsession with the return.

Hunted and hunting the teeth remember more than I wish to know.

So many swigs from the skull cup? *Is it me it was?*

Meditation is not sterilization.

The furthest away is the oldest to be new.

This is as real as beyond my capacity.

Poetry is a tongue bath on the path of deconditioning.

Suck the lyric back in.

Allow me to pour another cup of emotion.

Feeling the way home with your heart in your throat *tells a tale on you.*

You feel yourself inside the thing saying so far into your life sentence.

Spore words spook by night.

The sense of person is an inevitable outcome variably fateful.

Can't help speaking to alternate listening.

Local vehicles *will* old name chariots and end up purveyors of ancient babblers.

Modal verb magics.

Word spores moving you on where home's anywhere you can.

I listen therefore I'm not me.

What gets through is about what you're ready to think it is.

Wise thighs. Sleight of grip.

Scent of word woman rising from the gap is oft reported in this situation.

How big the between begins the Beguine. Women of the way wayward.

In the lapse of sense she is moving to whiteout thinking.

Singing along tails her and you are her trail.

Note to the self: poetry is a deconditioning agent working for goddess knows who.

In the dark the planet is blackboard notation.

The good life starts its talking in its rainforest.

Marguerite is burning flashes in the place of reference.

Disappearance is the fate of verbal objects.

Residue is dance before you know it. *Romance!*

Me I go for the chemistry.

The order of statement is matrimonial.

There's lush room at the crossroads the devil cannot find.

Any suggestion of persons living or dead is not the view of management.

Raw desire is literally standing revealed in its alphabet.

It's the view of itself here and there.

I'm speaking to the open spaces.

My voice hears you listening futurewise.

Hands speak by realizing their nature as verbs.

Even mind alone mates with an other in nowhere but here.

This is not a convenience.

It's a split in itself. Lingual cleaving.

That anything can be said anywhere at once tells the moment its crux.

Between coupling is watching the self-performing dakini dance.

The mother tongue is a lurid development in quantum entanglement.

A line is waiting for the jolt from its elsewhere.

There is a difference in poetry as from law to dream and place to non-place.

The threshold is the point of greatest distance from everything at once.

Mind forgets how to sit.

Make no mistake Mother Tongue is enjoying her lurid entangling.

She sleeps with us all at once.

My hand reminds me through you, I'm hearing myself say.

And hearing back: *intelligence is playing with itself like it or not.*

World behind is world surround in disguise.

Dreaming flame as female force you know the thought true is always getting away.

Her smile proves the hidden face just now appearing.

She takes each word into her mouth and licks it until it means one world more.

The trace clinging to the lingo is syntactic in its singularity aware.

She has taught me not to hate my bad education that left language free.

Form is what the statement does behind my back.

I'm left playing with my zero and the world pressing in from surround.

My life feels guided from attachment to attachment blocking the view of the pit.

The altered state is invisible in the thing altering.

Letting go too soon you lose your way in nevernever mind.

It's warmer up close empty than I dare think.

Freed attention follows syntax into its dark gaps touching down only undertime.

Lines are never really straight and won't target.

Poem fails, back to chaos. Relief.

I left myself standing outside the door of the church of myself.

Not born to worship or be worshiped but to hold spectacular options apart.

Awaiting the force of a lingual afterglow I catch a trace that never stops gesturing.

In the body syntactic the mouth is a verb.

I never know what I'm saying until I return hunting down happiness.

What makes her seem to run in reverse?

The love in holding back saying holds further in.

All things said here are questions from the blue.

I know it speaks true when the timbre hits the ground with a certain *hum.*

Known in saying as she knows me in smiling off-center.

Faint flow requires study, how the heart grows variable.

Charged words learn to dump fuel in flight.

They say *Do what we are doing.*

It sounds otherworldly telling it straight.

This is not my language suddenly signifies what is real.

Thinking objects. It says itself that you can't interpret. Edging back to center.

We have landed.

Word shadows to follow — mapping starting underfoot. Hail Thoreau!

The real in the territory traveled remains strange.

The longing to contact the same other is for the sake of other sameness.

I'm blowing the whistle on tooting my horn as she passes.

Here it comes again: *We have not yet sat all the way down.*

Poetry is a cover-up.

Refusal to know the poet is female projects her out to muse.

Closed history spoils.

Fear is other people.

The god only is in saying lay off the judging that's for me to do.

The concept *right* is not half as right as it thinks.

This stops short of lying paradoxically.

A line never drops its accent.

Its only translation is crossing tongues.

The poem is not good at other languages.

On this model incarnation is a spirited maneuver to attract intensities.

Pulsed but uncompelled, false without the swell.

I don't believe in goblins but I'm worried they might believe in me.

I keep a nickel in my pocket like a foreign term corrupting my verbal ore.

Language is traced through with belief.

Mind tricks. Syntax sculpts.

No safer in numbers than in my not my mind.

Poetics does not breed certainty, paradoxically.

Hang back before you wise up.

Content is what shows up in the cross-flares.

The poem is person to person via whatever or not at all.

Watch the word be invasive species taking hold where mind feels most free.

Language language everywhere nor any a thought to think.

It riddles but is not one.

The word is as much a thing as the thing it thinks to be.

Spokes for walking mind roll backwards against staged seeing.

Any readable superinterposition textifies to quantum mind sex.

Restless release shall not cease till mind recalls sitting all the way down.

Self knowing is what *I* does for the things around me.

Spying at large is for opening minds.

One stone knows nothing but its other stone unsettles.

Art stops the line from telling more than it knows.

The crux of the throbbing *pains through* to undertime.

No stone unturned upsets the mind set of all sets.

My life is the page where a writing stages.

Lector phages form afar.

One more sunrise across the field of syllables pulsing now toward these words.

Horizon in place, I say to birth in feedback, *the river tongues*.

"What's an artist but a self-tuning human set loose on his own recognizance?"

At long last we've got the answers on the run.

E.g.: *I'm here tracking down repressions of gravity.*

I'm a floater and my fear is getting away prematurely.

I offer poly-pulse-rhythms with continuous availability of zero point sourcing.

The ontological status of free-floating speculation is up for grabs.

I'm listening with my own fears.

Bodhisattvas at the heart of the budding flame in our time.

Nature in her nature flashes to free.

Things said say the more they say themselves all the way down.

I admit I can't get the mood right.

The Scarlet Pimpernel's my quantum hero, seek him here, there, everywhere.

We proceed in the name of revolution, as time goes under the wheel. Tears.

Even if I could tell you how to feel I wouldn't dare for fear of coercive art.

Just keep talking until she talks.

Got a look in the mirror, finally, and I'm relieved, it's not me.

Got tension? give birth.

Language is just another act like you.

Are they more afraid that this is real or that it is not?

I'm writing at the between space calling on the cross eyes.

A formal system perpetuates the expectation of return.

On the other hand there is a handdown intention to be in love.

This no how disproves breaking apart on the spot.

The music is the close cut around the rough corners.

Alter the angle of listening wherever a terrible beauty is born.

Soon enough the numbers calm down knowing we lose the will to use them.

Skip back a thought.

Watch the fray. Spectacular.

Touch torn feral is the heart of the song.

Residual lament for the lost foreskin. Lost tear in sound.

I'm tracking the long fate of bareheaded desire.

Music of the emptying field, felt syllables pulsing toward words to come.

It's how the horizon holds in place to travel rough.

Thought process careful not to be followed never pretends to know whodunit.

I'm leveling with you as of now.

There's no hope without shadows to give a face its cut.

A whole sense of the real gets its start with closer shaves.

I've been learning to talk straight—via tribulation of the tongue let free.

One word echoes for a lifetime.

I seem to be just making this up yet the mirror says otherwise.

Ringing true requires picking up the phone.

A riddle to diddle is soundly not the middle is half imaginable.

No doubt the tone to hone is closer to the bone.

I'm being watched by the watcher watching the watcher.

I wrestle with belief in witches, fearing the turn erotic.

When will she let be free to see?

She's waiting inside.

I hear her coming.

Joy cut to the bone is sounding like an actual voice.

Her tone turns on a pivot in the crux.

It takes shaved phonation to get her tale so far through.

I turn on out of myself to make ready for a world of difference.

She's a plant in my dream of tricks and someone is telling me covertly *pick her*.

Identity is the way the words flicker in a waking sentence.

It's a medium when it knows.

Hard to miss the reflection convexly mirroring what she sees in me.

I am who rides the curve listening.

Words speaking for themselves is what is being let.

Syntax is ultimately a danger first to itself.

We're focused inadvertently on incidental infrastructure.

From here to there and back tracks.

The game is to hang close to the ridge of the mouth, rider on the wind.

I'm wafting, no doubt, and wonder if there is kite thinking.

Something is not getting done.

A wind is many winds woven.

I'm thinking with a string in a state of lace.

I'm tuning to get a hold hearing under the roar.

I don't know why it's so important to follow the thread as if staying on a road.

If I affirm *it just is* it's a response to self-involved anxiety in the speaking.

There's proof after all that a road exists — in the proving.

Feeling freer is a turn of phrase still turning.

Clouds talk to mind like clay to hands and stone to stone behanded.

It's almost impossible to speak with the integrity of life waking on the spot.

I can admit it's me in that it thinks with my mind.

This is not necessarily its best choice, thinking in advance.

But that the woman inside have her say I can't say to play.

Living tastes.

I negotiate intensities. More's more by a lot.

Music is the stringing in the longing.

Unless you get it a life there is no other there.

Wonder who is doing the thinking in the ecstasy of absence.

The last step in a triad is over a newly conceived edge.

It thinks the way I don't know how.

Hearing bespeaks my keeping up.

Not thinking to know it the thing's found thinking within it.

Skipping the riddle the punch folds in.

I'm relieved to be in the dark of the turn on in, further yet.

There's rhythmic backslide, a slip back in, signing back in place.

Reflective dissipation tracks its loss of heat as we speak, and it revives.

I'm waking up the more I address you in these unknown or forbidden ways.

Continuous involution of the sentence is discouraged where I come from.

I'm speaking now in the middle run.

This memorializes readiness at long last to leave the meaning ajar.

I'm writing my will in order to understand power.

I have nothing more to say nor am I in a position to hold back at the end of any line.

If you've come this far you know we're changing form on the go.

Mind registers loss of local intent the more it lets be unknown happily.

A sentence gets truer the roomier the syntactic corners reserved for doubt.

Dancing in the aisles is a strategy of indirection called fun.

The analog is happiness between words and ecstasy between letters.

Suddenly I'm willing to be one of the dancers as though mushrooms had legs.

Time from this perspective is musical measure.

Nevertheless I can't seem to stop grating against the pulse.

Dreaming wormholes offers a way through language, time driven.

The longing is so long it leads through cracks in time not yet happening.

The act joining us here is connecting in undertime and the rapids still unnoticed.

The aforeconceived dancing crosses where there's traffic, danger, *attention!*

Like a werewolf I don't believe in myself but under pressure of strange desire.

It feels like a jungle in here, to state the inside of the otherside at hand.

I get the picture as one morph resonates with another, watch the birds.

It has to happen to be told.

This I know happens to be telling, there's a feel of word forming strangely.

Why do I care that everywhere things should speak as they do, yet I do.

Words, birds.

The mouth feels an action coming from behind.

Something gets a running start from downunder.

Irruption from the bush is a species of fire wings.

This is a launch midway in the journey of our morphery. Birding.

Purgatory may not be the best name for the middle zone though it's purging.

Middle earth bespeaks a first urge.

The surge is the next middle up like writing lefty.

It feeds left out.

Saying anything has a plumb line to fall through.

Any getting true is returning from the bottom up.

It calls itself up from its dead.

woman at the heart of it all

for Susan

You know it's your time.

If you feel it it's yours.

It makes you throw your arms around.

Nature talks too much as anyone living here knows.

Who has *time* for everything when everything is turning out before?

You take it at an angle and turning around inside.

Not much can be said in general, personally speaking, and there's a noise factor.

The tree is better listening, and now we're listening better.

I have to wait for the moment when I can be here all around.

Thoughts have sex without telling you.

Permission immemorial is not granted.

The tongue that finds its poem approaches liquidity.

Words revealing their secrets trick out a lost world.

The timing is layering up. It feels like your turn.

She plays with the head a word at a time to remix your motives.

The most sexually active language is not talking about sex.

Poetry is made at the edge of running language.

Language ready to come through here is experienced beyond my means.

I would catch it as it curves in on itself, it cuts so close to the ear.

I'm here searching out the source of what is scratching at my window.

The world wants to know its names.
It lets you speak so it can speak unnoticed.
Stuff comes up from the bottom because it's stirring to be here.

It feels you feeling your way around.
Life's dramatic content is safe in the adjoining room.
You find it hard to believe. Getting stirred.

Freedom to declare the thing itself as only it can imagine is outside ken.
The land of milk and honey is knowing biblically under singular circumstances.
Thank mind doctoring for the uncanny path to weirdish fateful speaking.

The tongue turns as a stepping stone in the shifting weight of the words heard.
The poem avoids the trap of gender by declaring itself female in my hands.
Hands signal from the center moving as the crux excites.

You can sense her setting mirror neurons humming a new tune, still to be heard.
It's only her when it's never been said and still hasn't quite.
What you are hearing has no choice but to have never been.

She's only asking that I read her beyond distinction, even as I pass it all on.
I'm left talking to language as if she's standing there disrobing.
The undercurrent is barely being able to wait.

The dream catches me on fire.

I go to the only place I can hear the half-lost language of a still lost land.
New words are the earth's last effort at a comeback.
Possible sayings, probable loves.

Please get my history off the cross nailed down with dates.
There she goes pushing the sky behind in an act of my perception.
I hope you're not understanding me just because I'm coming down.

Let's not go too heavy on the mental groping.
I'm minded to tell you what I've never thought before.
This is just between us.

There's nowhere else not here.
She makes me stop making sense but not sensing.
I found myself a big sensory organ of the mind.

Reading rooted is double vision.
An animate tongue is self watching.
Do you get the feeling you're being looked through a word at a time?

I'm less real today than yesterday, I dreamed vividly in between.

All the stark images got squeezed out of view today.

Language truth is a lightning strike.

It's not an it.

How do you know a poem's coming but the probability clouds are forming.

Something's ready to speak and no telling what.

It keeps its sex life secret.

My poem not mine accepts to be your projection.

It comes with a verbal slide rule.

Not honing my individuation but the angel's on the fly.

The poetics of possible identity knows the space has its own intelligence.

I'm not the author of my dreams but their stopover.

Lognosis is not the name it goes by.

Portrait of the artist as just himself is looking through the window starkly.

Resonance is radial.

Getting this far's experienced language.

I talk to the dream, not to the person.

Resonance is romance among things within hearing.

Mind follows the path you name.

The waking medicine is cracking jokes again.

Strange factors hollow out these resonating minded spaces.

The funny faces of one story may tear your throat out in another.

Trust nothing.

Identity's assumed.

What you found along the way stands out in intelligent space.

Language workers and sex workers share the problematic of staying in the body.

Guilt by association is too attractive to avoid.

Words flee from the hand on the knee. Scare easily.

Anything trusts to be anywhere.

If the name torques the path torques.

A true line leaves space to resume identity willy-nilly.

Follow the bouncing thought.

It's not an it even to itself.

Mind shows when the flow is knowing.

Portrait of the artist as just herself's where the blank lets me in.

Intimacy is self-sensing secret.

I write to come back to myself as I've never been.

The middle is linear suspension with evident gaps hungry for sense.

Marking the page without permission is transgression.

The motivation to keep it going to get it right is a subtle matter unto materia.

To say I'm a man of desire is to say human.

When you hear *woman* you know no title tells the more you are.

Proof negative is the further of identity.

The sense of collaborating through extracorporeal epidermal mind silk heartens.

Muse stands in for what can never be asserted and rarely attested.

The true tune's as much behind as before me, down under and rising.

I know it's here when I wonder how to ride.

From across a space mindful of itself but no good manners tasty word hits tongue.

I can't pray but it prays for me.

I stand behind no statement here for I'm still before.

I'm rational like wartime ration.

Wondering what it means is the origin of silence.

I live at the beginning of my life, which is now.

Self is a closet case.

No one speaks from desire as it continuously happens.

She dreamt I painted her face green—how queer is exotic.

Every moment's an object I can walk around when I wake up in time.

A party, she said, is where people enjoy confusion as to who should be licked or not.

Language finds itself in the closet.

The queer inside proves time's not equal in distribution.

A solitary right knows itself to be.

If we could read each other's mind the world would reformulate by the moment.

Self-true language is always foreign.

The living will says resuscitate without knowing what is being said.

Question is beyond question from the start, which is now.

If you can't feel the feeling pull back in time.

Poetry's getting out of the way of inexperienced primordial charge.

Good times are rolling as we speak.

Why the anxiety if origin is yet to be.

I was alone feeling her hand reaching around me from behind having just dreamt.
Can you think *identifying with the text it has sex* without reservations?
In the dream her dangling modifier appearing, it was me.

This is how identity works by grammatical confusion and inherent skullduggery.
Have you identified your line yet so you can say it was lost and now is found?

Now is found wanting.
Meditating the mind thinks in its moment without precedent.
The thing said is a thing to circumambulate. Slowing but not always.

The phrase entering yesterday in my notebook showing up here teaches hyperlocal.
There's no other way to say it but what it does.

Now is found. I'm right over here.
Language says so.

It doubles for the place to be.
That's how different it is now that it sits across from itself and you.

Poetics you could say is the whole materia of arrangement.
This is as close as we get is forewarned in the matter of relationship.

Please come closer.
I've been waiting to hear these words all my life, which is now.

Re: this life thing don't you think it has something better to do than be regular?

It doesn't matter how I am on the outside, which is confusing.

How I'm brought together with myself translates not except for sudden leaps over.

A call of the wild I call it in private.

Sounds like a woman's voice despite thinking it's me.

The grammar's not so good in the sense of vegetables turning color at the market.

You can't judge what is judging itself.

The difficulty is learning its language in time to know it in time.

The only way to do it *is as* it speaks to itself.

Poetry has always known it was overhearing.

This is *nothing* new.

You've got its whole wide tongue in your hand.

The bird alights on a hidden sentence.

The grammar is that you see it at all.

So the restraint built into the occasion is consequentially verbal.

This is the dharma of the misplaced referent.

It won't be tracked outside its occasion.

It lacks while still on track.

You. Or me.

The presumption a someone is trying to reach us is gratuitous, wishful, unavoidable.
Be more vivid.

You just have to think about her speaking, breathing audible in writing backwards.
You know she belongs to you as you belong to earth plus where you come from.
Why this hour is how it feels to ask at dawn as in why life at all.

Sometimes identifying with the text it has sex, causally intimate.
It explains the attraction of otherwise ordinary signs.
I'm only asking with backseat driver humility to attend as language speaks for itself.

The rhythm is inseparable from finger spelling words.
Speed is another matter. Unto materia.
Back to the roots non-separate from the flowers, the sexual parts, innumerable.

The plant stops making sense at the stage of the flower.
The flow turns to air, breathably.
This is what words do departing the lips for heat-seeking ears.

Art is that your hands are in the dirt proving mind is following.
How did we get here is always the question and need not be asked.
Text is a dimension among many and poetry is its level of self-selection.

Retreat in the poem to find your way in the dark.
Raven light.

Don't say I said this but you say it for yourself.
I couldn't believe she was saying this.

On the other hand I couldn't be here unless I was different from myself.
Only quote this when not making a point.

The poem is not responsible for its readability but it must leave open tactility.
Pick yourself up at line beginning and let yourself down at the end is, say, rhythm A.
Begin as in the middle, rhythm M, or indifferently with respect to position, rhythm X.

How many directions it's allowed to dance stands for letting orientation loose.
What's ahead on Track One has not been announced stands for poetic hazard.
I stand for her.

Dancing on Track One is all I've learned here but never how.
If it weren't on schedule although there is no schedule we wouldn't still be together.
Poetics is attestation to the fact.

The lineaments are loosening.
Gratification self-conceives.
Locomote in place as the planet turns round in spiraling solarity.

Someone is saying something to someone right here.
It's pointless to say a compass points unless at itself from behind.
Being makes rounds.

The birth of saying forefronts the sharp cry as if in pain or ecstasy.

Exciting to think is the preeminent life thing as the unthinkable thing.

I'm overexcited is how I get here.

"I'm just drawn this way" indicates showing up is medium specific.

Why does one only know what is being said as in a rearview mirror?

Poetry is overhearing at the speed of sound late yet getting into step at zero point.

Who taught you to dance is the traditional question for this traditionary questing.

An actual leaf leaves its matrix in place.

A word carries out its -typal source fix regardless of punctuation.

These two lines agree in the sense of nature and mother.

I wear my heart on my syllable.

The practice is asking how it feels riding in a star cart and she's never out of view.

I couldn't begin to know her until I lost track of where I was and then who, who.

To read is to enter the condition as it is without knowing it.

The pulse is syllabic and hooting accordingly backtracks to the tongue itself.

I feel myself dropping down along the lines of roots.

The sense of gravity in the midst of significant winds registers rebound, holes.

Catching onto to itself stays within lingual bounds.

Getting more primordial as the days hum by.

Relief is touching the word like a compact animal, giving off warm waves.

What I didn't say's what I meant to say.

The gap won't let me go.

Funnily is getting to speak at all.

If I saw myself I'd have to laugh.

The sadness of dates is upon us.

Laughing creates a space in which to weep in advance, sounding akin.

In a long breath there may be no death.

Why is the poem still here rather than meeting on the outside.

Long enough, deathless enough, the more breathless.

It wants to know so it makes a show.

It has words for what is happening in advance.

It knows nothing until now left open.

A line is not one-way like a hole.

Turn at the pulse and still feel back.

The threshold of clarity is a turning point with lumens.

You can sense when the words are watching where they're going.

They seed sentences to come and yet retain.

Wondering why you were ever born or what is the function of the text.

If it all blew away was it worth it anyway?

Are there still dragons in real words?

Tunnel drawing looks straight through end to end no matter how many curves.

Vital questions wormhole.

Knowing you're off energizes proprioceptively.

Circulating force in an interruptive life seeds the field as we speak.

The face in the cloud is the future ancient.

Modular linear is telling tales on time.

Are triplets trigrams or more babies crying than I have arms?

Good questions go both ways, down will come baby cradle and all, still falling out.

Speaking in 3s, three souls in one breast, stands for what I stand for and sits down.

Lustration of the lingual fields is ancient starting now.

You're aboard this vehicle out of desire for the journey downstream, self named.

The stream like the dream is self dividing along the way.

To promote hope without knowing it knows where it's going is dogma.

Two lobes, two globes, plus untold off rimes to mind all worlds.

Dante forever beholding Beatrice in the starcart lustrates the surround.

This is only ancient in the moment casting a shadow where the line cuts deep.

If there's a poem to welcome me to the other side it differs from itself at every turn.

Imagine a handle on the soul.

Call back to the adventure, lift the cover up, show the naked need, get wet.

I can't help talking to myself as though no one will talk to me.

The intimate cost, a flowing element, liquid crystal, the unknown sense downunder.

We want it all because it all wants us.

This is what is wanting.

A realization steps long and I lurch heart first.

We're in this together and can't admit it, such is the danger at hand.

She keeps her distance in Dante and all works that know longing interminable.

The poem is the trick that calls the poet out to where denial fails.

It invents a world that's always already there covered over.

I dream a music's ravishing dakinis, gentle beyond the fiercest fire.

She teaches a poetics beyond caring, an ecstasy of wanting.

Where there are two hands there are two musics.

There's barely a word that never reaches double.

Born to teach reaching.

Here we go fighting background dualism while smiling at foreground dogma.

Watch the zero dance for where you are gone.

I have invited a council of elders into my body to mind their invisibles.

We're here rounding off identity.
Pressed-in life is coming out to get home in these newly emptied rooms.
Letting be called back makes anywhere nowhere but here.

A message here waits to be sent, patient with the passions of request.

Music is the enemy of already knowing.
(No experts inside.)
Verbal objects do not unite except in the sense of tryst.

Consciousness is what keeps contraries interactive, otherwise war.
As any doublebrained being knows, hands are born to grow independent.
There is secret resonance of the irreconcilable.

I'm making your portrait with two hands to keep the peace in your face.
The mouth is the organ that plays itself.
The tongue the one always getting out and never.

The overtone is between takes.
Between doublings, music, music.
Sense and sensation inseparate in the tunneling.

Sound touches, music consorts.

Tapping fingers for haptic harmony is a slogan on the run.

A line is scored space to find a music.

The center of buoyancy shifts according to vessel volume and all out speed.

A sea is axial for any body reading space.

Walking on water is a familiar mental option.

Freedom without commitment is drift.

Is philosophy seaworthy in climatologically daunting weather?

Thought here is a placeholder or else a prison cell.

The last supper is great in name only.

It's hard to take note of site specifics facing execution.

Dangling reference is male intellect astray at long last.

This is what we've been waiting for where *this* is the shakily open set.

Standing outside looking in I see myself intimately at a remove.

No bars held.

Between scientist and voyeur there is no safe boundary.

Music of the peers peering.

Grammar is a language kit good for getting started. Flat before flat out.

I'm reminding myself like retreading. Tactile syntactics.

There's no other way to say anything true but original.

I hear a voice as if shouted from a passing vehicle, think Dante, then read it back.

Myth of freedom, myth of originality, excellence in orientation.

I know the text is mine when I don't quite recognize the next line.

No comfort zone, so lay on back, sweat the syllables to speak like you.

Perspective is surreal by nature.

I have panicked in dreams of staying afloat too long, but why think that here?

Walking on water is proprioceptive porn.

Spread the legs temporal with uplift.

Bite the bone with retention, know first the inner life of small feral animals.

Once a camera, always a camera somewhere, and we edit as we go.

A shift in view excites to inaction.

It gets harder to justify leaving inner children home alone.

No killing over spilled milk.

A midline crisis is scale invariant.

The ecstasy is standing beside from the inside out, enminding surroundings.

Page, book, house, attack on the surface that releases.

The lick of a lack is just like it sounds.

I was lost and I'm not found, and learning to like it that way.

Taking it as it comes teaches its singular logic.

It's difficult to keep pulling back my other foot still walking out of time.

Harder and harder to fête the thing well thought, well said, timed to a stop.
Better thought sloughed off for a possible now more bare than the will to affirm.
A line affords metagender acts of tongue even while *saying her.*

Raw heart in a flash of the thing now known no longer denied.
I try hard not to write it rough but the force is from behind.
The order erupts from the middle as a head pushes through like tongues.

Attitudes are moments in a violent flow, shapes in flood.
The possible stays raw.
Birth incurs.

Mastery and mystery sound more alike than they are.

The question what is poetry asks itself differently daily.
Advancing by hand scratching letters feels the texture of mouth eros.
Reading in the act finds a blood pulse from the inside élan.

The poem is of every day where every is only now.
Looking through the instant window sees farther yet in no time.
I trip over my own words when I forget they're not only mine.

Embodying along a line transgresses my unnoticed unknowns.

Pressing up against this surface makes it feel your tongue.

I'm writing this all the way down.

Pen in teeth. Cursive in the head swerve. The thought the feel in how it gets up.

She gets under my skin is literal in knowing the book I am in here.

Inspiration by letters licking your lips.

Saying it's secret makes it secret but you still might know it, secretly.

If you say I said this I won't deny it but I might be confused for a space.

Recall recreates.

Memory is an out of body experience.

Tingling in the extremities is alarming, transitive like subtle violent reminding.

This is a talk channel of which we speak.

It came to light, sound, body in a dream payphone call, call back, pay back.

Texture of sound, surface, syntax, text qualia, indifferently.

Belonging to body thinking is never only before.

We're not so far apart.

Gut sense text wise.

A long true tale is too tall to tell let alone follow.

In dream walking the plank saw how ego's thrust cuts itself off in the end.

More and more words are on the run.

Letting loose with no engagement transmigrates, no rudder.

If prediction turns out to be counterproductive it may be art.

This is a word run.

There are levels of disengagement in memorializing.

Connecting is not *all* in the body's cursive swerve.

Writing things are circling each other, now observing, now leering.

Running verbals on the double.

Ambiguity means another language is trying to get a word in.

Knock knock. Who's there? That's my question.

Laughing cries for me in secret.

A definite bounding line is that a thing is in its skin.

Calligraphs of the turning mind, word spin, being talks round.

Facing is never away, neither is it a way.

I begin to understand being blown away.

No time is ever not here.

The run of the word tells me how I'm running.

Stomach growling from line to line retains a wild.

Aswim in doubt is failing to shore.

AWOL in denial, not desire.

Fantasy is social media on the sly, avid joining through cracks in the wall.

Thank you for the lyric showing me how I can't talk.

We've come here to disjoin in marriage.

This makes me hear *carriage* as how I go along side by side in step syllabic.

In the mirror my haircloth sheath has a jewel in hiding so I'm sane.

This is a temporary denial zone.

More air *then* more light.

Triumph is funereal.

If I say *shunya* I'm dropping names.

Teaching is and not.

The part that is helps me find my way to the end of the line and not beyond.

I'm participating in the delay in turnover. What's not, yet here.

So what if my poem is not by me or anyone who goes by the name.

I'm a straggler by choice.

No force but voice at source.

I was born yesterday and it's not over yet.

I read everything as though it just wrote through me.

The self of self-reference cannot perceive its own liberation.

Skip analogy like Whitman's voice unto itself's like Lao-tzu's cloud through a gate.

There is a poetics of skipping names over water.

Accordingly fireside reverie is a mid-line phenomenon.

Intelligence in sexual precision happily models the future poem.

We've got the wrong idea about everything.

We come here to feel all the way through. Unwind choice.

The intelligence hereby evaded is evasive.

The count of three is breathing; still here, still breathing.

This helps me enmind my house as I enwind my source.

No word leaves its root behind but hides it from you till she trusts you.

Pulsive rhythm rides a wave through cross currents, erratic erotic.

Etymophonics studies roots talking crazy when outed.

The self of self-reference erodes in viewing.

Writing diminishing is corrosive.

New mind in dark places is popping up everywhere by the syllable.

Zero dances for you alone and a sleepless mind.

TABLE OF TITLES

About the Author

George Quasha is a poet, artist, writer and musician working in mediums in which he explores certain principles active within composition. The primary medium is language, but principles discovered there are active also in sculpture, drawing, video, sound, and performance. A tri-partite principle is axial/liminal/configurative, discussed in *Axial Stones: An Art of Precarious Balance*, foreword by Carter Ratcliff (North Atlantic Books: Berkeley, 2006) and *An Art of Limina: Gary Hill's Works and Writings*, with Charles Stein; foreword by Lynne Cooke (Ediciones Polígrafa: Barcelona, 2009).

Solo exhibitions of axial stones, drawings and video include the Baumgartner Gallery in New York (Chelsea), the Slought Foundation in Philadelphia, and at the Samuel Dorsky Museum of Art at SUNY New Paltz.

The first of nine volumes of preverbs published was *Verbal Paradise (preverbs)* (Zasterle Press: Tenerife, Spain, 2011) with two others are projected for 2015: *The Daimon of the Moment (preverbs)* (Talisman House Press) and *Things Done for Themselves (preverbs)* (Marsh Hawk Press). Titled preverbs series are also appearing in chapbooks, to date: *Scorned Beauty Comes Up From Behind* (2012) and *Speaking Animate* (2014) (Between Editions: Barrytown, NY).

Other poetry includes: *Somapoetics* [1-58]: Book One (first-fifth series) (1973), *Word-Yum: Somapoetics 64-69* (seventh series) (1974); *Giving the Lily Back Her Hands* (1979); and *Ainu Dreams* (1999). Anthologies: *America a Prophecy: A New Reading of American Poetry from Pre-Columbian Times to the Present* [with Jerome Rothenberg](Random House, 1973; Station Hill of Barrytown, 2013); *Open Poetry: Four Anthologies of Expanded Poems* [with Ronald Gross] (Simon & Schuster, 1973); *An Active Anthology* [with Susan Quasha] (Sumac Press, 1974); *The Station Hill Blanchot Reader* [with Charles Stein] (1998).

Awards include a Guggenheim Fellowship in video art and an NEA Fellowship in poetry.

The video work **art is/music is/poetry is:** *Speaking Portraits* records over 1000 artists, poets, and composers (in 11 countries) saying what in their view art is. Exhibitions of this and other works include the Snite Museum of Art (University of Notre Dame), White Box (NYC), the Samuel Dorsky Museum (SUNY New Paltz), and biennials (Wroclaw, Poland; Geneva, Switzerland; Kingston, New York).

A 30-year performance collaboration continues with Gary Hill and Charles Stein, and more recently with David Arner and John Beaulieu. **See quasha.com.**

CPSIA information can be obtained at www.ICGtesting.com
Printed in the USA
LVOW11s2140160416

483926LV00001B/20/P